The Craft of Silversmithing

The Craft of Silversmithing

Techniques, Projects, Inspiration

Alex Austin

LARK BOOKS

A Division of
Sterling Publishing Co., Inc.
New York

The Library of Congress has cataloged the hardcover edition as follows:

Austin, Alex P.
    The craft of silversmithing : techniques, projects, inspiration / Alex
P. Austin.
        p. cm.
    Includes index.
    ISBN 1-57990-449-1 (hardcover)
    1. Jewelry making. 2. Silverwork. I. Title.
    2004
    739.2'3--dc22

                                        2003022197

10 9 8 7 6 5 4 3 2 1

Published by Lark Books, a division of
Sterling Publishing Co., Inc.
387 Park Avenue South, New York, N.Y. 10016

First Paperback Edition 2007
© 2004, Alex Austin

Distributed in Canada by Sterling Publishing,
c/o Canadian Manda Group, 165 Dufferin Street
Toronto, Ontario, Canada M6K 3H6

Distributed in the United Kingdom by GMC Distribution Services,
Castle Place, 166 High Street, Lewes, East Sussex, England BN7 1XU

Distributed in Australia by Capricorn Link (Australia) Pty Ltd.,
P.O. Box 704, Windsor, NSW 2756 Australia

If you have questions or comments about this book, please contact:
Lark Books
67 Broadway
Asheville, NC 28801
(828) 253-0467

Manufactured in China

ISBN 13: 978-1-57990-449-4 (hardcover) 978-1-60059-131-0 (paperback)
ISBN 10: 1-57990-449-1 (hardcover) 1-60059-131-0 (paperback)

For information about custom editions, special sales, premium and corporate
purchases, please contact Sterling Special Sales Department at 800-805-5489
or specialsales@sterlingpub.com.

EDITOR:
Marthe Le Van

ART DIRECTOR:
Kristi Pfeffer

PHOTOGRAPHER:
Steve Mann

COVER DESIGNER:
Barbara Zaretsky

ILLUSTRATOR:
Orrin Lundgren

ASSISTANT EDITOR:
Nathalie Mornu

ASSOCIATE ART DIRECTOR:
Shannon Yokeley

EDITORIAL ASSISTANCE:
Delores Gosnell

ART PRODUCTION:
Jessy Mauney

EDITORIAL INTERN:
Ryan Sniatecki

Contents

Introduction

As a silversmith, my task is surprisingly straightforward. I transform flat pieces of sheet metal into useful objects with different hammers, stakes, and other simple tools. Metal is wonderfully malleable and can be crafted into so many things. You can create beautiful objects to use everyday or to give to friends and family. All you need is an understanding of the basic tools and techniques of silversmithing. My goal with this book has been to make these topics accessible and the process approachable for beginning and experienced metalworkers alike. Covering every aspect of silversmithing in one book, however, would be too formidable a task, even for myself. What I've done instead is to provide you with a practical introduction to silversmithing so you can start exploring it right away.

Silversmithing was an early addiction for me, and one that I've never been able to shake. It started with my love for tools, specifically my father's woodworking tools, which I snuck into the basement to use as a child. That led me to a summer working in a variety of art studios. It was an absolutely wonderful time. To a tool-obsessed child like myself, the well-stocked woodshop was a dream come true, but the instructor felt I was too young to use the power tools. Constant pestering got me nowhere. This tactic did prove successful in the metals shop, however, where the teacher handed me a torch as he left the room and said in exasperation, "you are not my problem." Laws were different then, and a silversmith was born.

As I soon learned, before exploring silversmithing there are fundamental principles and practices you need to review and understand. I've compiled this essential information in the first chapter, The Basics. Here you'll find everything from a primer on understanding silver and how it behaves, to a step-by-step guide for setting up your own oxy-propane torch, to methods for obtaining (and maintaining!) your silver's highest shine. Clear instructions are supported with plenty of color photographs to make learning silversmithing easy and fun. Throughout the basics section, I've also inserted many hints and tips I've learned over the course of my career.

In the second chapter, The Projects, you'll find 20 of my favorite sterling silver designs. For each project I provide you with a comprehensive list of the materials, hammers, and other tools you'll need as well as step-by-step instructions and helpful photographs. From the beginning to the end of this chapter, the projects increase in complexity as your skills improve and you become more experienced.

Beginning silversmiths can create the handsome hammered Money Clip on page 50 or the Business Card Holder on page 59 in a single afternoon with only a few tools. Inter-

mediate silversmiths may want to try the Condiment Dish on page 76 or the Stone-Capped Baby Rattle on page 88 to develop their sinking and soldering skills. The Cocktail Shaker (page 116) and the Creamer & Sugar Bowl (page 123) require further skills, substantial labor, and additional time, but the extraordinary results are certainly worth the effort. Whenever you set out to create a silversmithing project, I hope you'll remember that it isn't a race. Enjoy what you're doing while you're doing it without placing time restrictions or excess pressure on yourself to finish quickly. By following this simple advice, you'll continue to love silversmithing while you learn it.

Like most silversmiths, I enjoy making functional things. There's something wonderfully satisfying knowing that people not only like but also use the unique objects I create. I also love a challenge and working with metal always provides one. Each day, I look forward to making metal move, to seeing what I may be able to accomplish, and to stretching my skills with the tools and materials. Much of silversmithing is not glamorous work. Sure, you get good and dirty. Of course, there are days when your muscles feel tired. And yes, there are times when you have to hammer or polish the same piece over and over, but the results can be so inspiring that I can't wait to get back into the studio and beat up another sheet of sterling silver. It's a pleasure to share my enthusiasm for and knowledge of the craft of silversmithing with you. It's a craft for everyone to practice and enjoy. I wish you great success.

The Basics

Understanding Silver & Silversmithing

To best understand the material and the process of silversmithing, you should first understand what it's *not*.

Silversmithing is not the hot-working of metal. Blacksmiths work with hot metal; silversmiths work with it cold. The difference is in the metals. Metals that are cold-worked are usually *nonferrous*, meaning they don't contain iron. Hot-worked metals are commonly *ferrous*, or iron-containing.

When they cool, ferrous metals have the ability to retain the motion and form given to them when hot. They also have a wide temperature range within which they're hot enough to move, but cool enough not to melt. These metals indicate their temperature by a change in color. This is an incredibly convenient way to track the heat of ferrous metal. Metals with a wide working temperature range are much more malleable when hot, so it makes more sense to move them then.

Nonferrous metals, such as sterling silver, do indicate temperature by color, but to a much limited degree. To most people, the color changes are almost invisible. These metals do not retain heat as well or as long. When hot, nonferrous metals have a smaller temperature range in which they're softer and ready to work. Since the window of opportunity to hot-work these metals is very brief and nearly impossible to distinguish by color, they're softened with heat, and then worked cold.

Heating Silver to Work It Cold?

To make a nonferrous metal malleable, you heat it up to an *annealing*, or softening, temperature. (For more information on annealing, see page 19.) This temperature varies slightly between the nonferrous metals, but all are close to 1,400° F (760° C). Sterling silver has a few ways of displaying its annealing temperature. One is commonly observed as the appearance of a "rose color" on its surface. I think it looks more like a dusty grey-rose. It's an incredibly subtle change. If your eyes can actually see the color rose, then you've probably overheated the material, stressing it to a point beyond its ideal annealing temperature.

There are tricks that make it easier to tell when a nonferrous metal has annealed. The best and most common is applying a material called *flux* to the metal. (For more information on flux, see page 31.)

Annealed silver is made even more malleable by *quenching*, or quickly cooling it in water rather than air-cooling it. This process can be tricky. If, for example, you overheat a piece of metal beyond the annealing temperature and then quench it, you stress the metal even

> **STERLING WORDS**
>
> WHETHER YOU'RE A BEGINNER OR AN EXPERIENCED SILVERSMITH, UNDERSTANDING YOUR MATERIALS IS ESSENTIAL.

Annealing silver

Quenching silver

more than the overheating alone. If you're a beginning silversmith, I recommend letting silver air cool until you develop a better feel for and understanding of the material.

Annealed silver has random spaces in its molecular structure, making it an outstanding metal with which to create artwork. Metals with tighter structures, fewer spaces and holes, are less malleable. A metal with tightly packed molecules won't want to move at all. When you anneal metal, its molecules start to bounce around, moving apart from each other and creating a looser structure. Quenching metal at this temperature freezes the molecules in this loose position. When you work the metal in this state, by hammering,

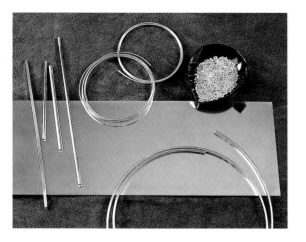

Left, clockwise from left: tubing, rod, wire, casting grain, sheet, more wire

Right: scrap silver pieces

Bottom left: various gauges of silver

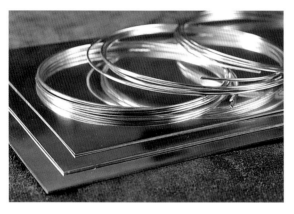

STERLING WORDS

WHEN BUYING SILVER, YOU'RE CHARGED BY ITS WEIGHT, NOT ITS DIMENSIONS.

pushing, or other means, its molecules have space to move. As you continue to work the metal, its molecules get compressed again and its structure tight, requiring re-annealing. This process of annealing, work-hardening, and re-annealing is pivotal to silversmithing.

Annealing silver is tricky work, but with practice your skills will improve. Here are several reasons to develop good technique.

• If you don't reach silver's annealing temperature, you won't get the molecular spacing required to make the metal flexible.

• If you hold the silver for too long at a hot or level annealing temperature, its molecules will start to stabilize, becoming harder as their spaces fill in and become more uniform.

• If you anneal silver at a temperature that's too high, the metal gets too close to melting, and its structure becomes more porous, often resulting in problems with cracking, pits, and brittleness.

• If you quench a piece of silver when it's over-annealed, you freeze it at this unstable point, making the silver more brittle. Although it may appear softer, it's also more fragile.

Buying Sterling Silver

Sterling silver is produced and sold in a variety of forms, such as sheet, wire, tubing, and casting grain. In this book, you'll be using sterling silver sheet and wire. There are standard methods for measuring these forms. For length and width, you can use common U.S. or metric measurements, but for thickness, silver is measured in gauge. Gauges inverse-

ly indicate the silver's thickness—the higher the gauge number, the thinner the metal. 18-gauge silver sheet metal is approximately 1 mm thick. A 20-gauge sheet is thinner, approximately .8 mm. 10-gauge sterling silver is really thick, approximately 2.6 mm, and 2 gauge is a good heavy silver ingot, approximately ¼ inch (6 mm) thick.

I'm often asked where and how I buy my silver. The best source for silver is through jewelry suppliers. If they don't carry what you need, they can likely refer you to another vendor. I most often purchase silver in sheet form. I also cast with leftover scraps to minimize wasting the material. All silver is useful for a silversmith. You can even return scrap silver to a refiner and receive a percentage of its price according to current market value.

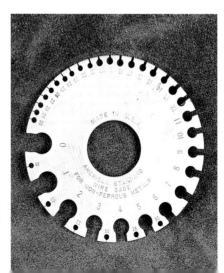

Hand tool for measuring sheet and wire gauge

Tools & Techniques for Forming Silver

Silversmiths use many tools to fabricate their work—I have over 7,000 pounds (3175 kg) of them—but, you'll be relieved to know you can start working with just a few. As your skills grow, you'll probably find more and more tools helpful to your silversmithing.

Transferring Designs onto Silver

To create some of the projects in this book, you'll first have to photocopy a design template, and then transfer its shape onto a sterling silver sheet. Often you can simply trace the form. I prefer tracing with a thin felt-tip pen and buy them in bulk for my studio. You can easily draw on silver with this type of pen, and the ink will hold very well. If you're working on a project with an intricate pierced and cutout design, you may want to affix the template directly to the silver sheet. You can use rubber cement to make this temporary attachment. Brush a thin layer of rubber cement on both the sheet metal and the back of the photocopied template. Carefully position the template on the metal. Let the rubber cement dry before sawing or piercing the metal.

Cutting Silver

Prior to beginning a project you'll often need to cut sterling silver sheets to specific dimensions. You can easily accomplish this with a jeweler's saw or metal shears.

Jeweler's Saw

A jeweler's saw is a tool necessary to every silversmithing studio. It looks and is used somewhat like a coping saw. You can purchase one from any jewelry supply store or catalog. Buy one with a frame that's at least 5 inches (12.7 cm) deep. This size is the most versatile. There are jeweler's saws with deeper frames, but these are more difficult to con-trol and require more skill to use. A beginning metalworker will break many more blades when using a deeper saw frame than when using a frame with a standard depth.

Jeweler's Saw Blades

Jeweler's saw blades are available in a variety of sizes. I most frequently use 3/0 blades. The popular 2/0 size is thicker and sturdier; whereas the 4/0 size is very thin and much too fragile for beginning metalsmiths. With experience, however, 4/0 blades are useful for sawing tight corners and intricate shapes. Jeweler's saw blades frequently break, especially when you're learning to saw metal. Fortunately, replacement blades are inexpensive, and you can buy them by the gross. Even seasoned metalworkers often have to change their saw blades because they

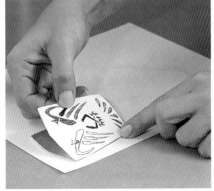

Brushing rubber cement on a photocopied template

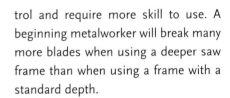

Positioning the template on the silver

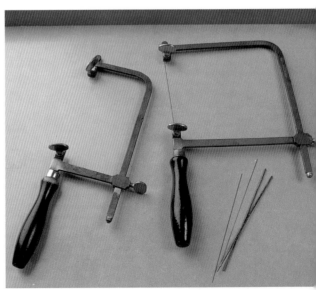

Jeweler's saws and saw blades

wear out, lose their teeth, and become incapable of cleanly cutting metal. I recommend learning to saw with a 2/0 blade.

Bench pin

Bench Pin

It's easiest to cut metal with a jeweler's saw at a jeweler's bench with a bench pin. A good bench pin is made from a wooden block and has a V shape cut into one end, allowing for support on both sides while metal is cut in the middle of the V. Some prefabricated pins may not have the V cutout. Most jeweler's benches are manufactured with a pin attached, but if you don't have one, you can easily make one from scratch with a C-clamp and a block of wood.

Installing a Saw Blade into a Saw Frame

1. Point the teeth of a single saw blade down toward the handle of the saw frame. If the teeth are too small for you to see, gently run your fingernail down the blade (see photo); then run your fingernail up the blade. When you feel it grabbing, you've discovered its teeth. Whichever direction is smooth to the touch is *down*.

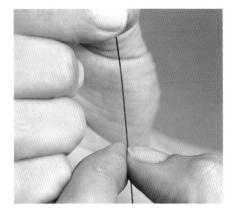

2. Loosen the nut at the top of the saw frame enough to accept the blade. Insert the top of the blade with its teeth pointing out and down. Tighten the nut as shown in the photo.

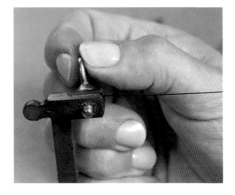

3. Loosen the nut at the bottom of the saw frame. Hold the top of the frame against your jeweler's bench or another sturdy work surface. Press into the saw's handle and compress the frame against your bench or work surface to create tension. (I use my sternum to compress the frame, but other metalworkers swear by using their hipbone. Using either of these body parts frees your hands to set the saw blade into the lower nut of the frame.) Place the bottom of the saw blade in the lower nut of the frame and tighten it (see photo). Gently back your body away from the frame to slowly release the compression. The blade is now taut in the frame.

Keeping the saw blade at a 90-degree angle to the silver

Keys to Sawing Metal

• Let the blade do the work. A jeweler's saw blade is small, thin, and delicate. It isn't designed to bear your weight while cutting metal, only to cut metal. You don't need to push hard on the frame.

• Always keep the saw blade at a 90-degree angle to the metal you're cutting. Twisting, angling, or shifting the blade while cutting exerts uneven pressure on it. This causes blades to break even faster.

• Use the entire length of the saw blade to cut the metal. Sawing with a full downward stroke uses the tool to its greatest advantage. Sawing with only a fraction of the blade's full length is inefficient, causes blades to break faster, and more quickly tires your arms.

• Move a saw blade forward into the metal only on the downward stroke. Never push a saw forward when making an upward stroke. If you think of the sawing motion a bit elliptically, this action may become more natural for you. As you practice sawing, it may help to pull the saw up and a tiny bit away from the metal on the upward stroke.

• To saw a curve or round a corner, move the metal, not the saw blade.

• Practice, practice, practice. You can develop and refine your sawing skills by cutting copper sheet prior to cutting sterling silver.

Metal Shears

Metal shears are excellent for quickly cutting straight lines. Heavy-duty shears come as a set and attach to a bench or worktable. Hand-held shears aren't as versatile as the bench-mounted type, and they can't cut thick metal. Metal shears aren't a required silversmithing tool. You'll be able to use a jeweler's saw to cut all of the metal for the projects in this book.

From top: heavy-duty shears, hand-held shears

Piercing Silver

You can make interior cutouts on a sterling silver sheet. These can range from simple shapes to complex decorative patterns. To use this technique you'll need to pierce the metal surface prior to sawing.

Drilling Silver

WHAT YOU NEED

Felt-tip pen
Practice sterling silver sheet
Swage block
Center punch*
Chasing hammer
Scrap wood block
Flexible shaft
Drill bit

This can be any kind of tool with a point on one end and a hammering surface on the opposite end. You'll use a center punch for making dimples prior to drilling holes.

WHAT YOU DO

1. Use a felt-tip pen to mark the silver surface at the location to be pierced, and then place the metal on top of the swage block (see page 25 for further information on swage blocks).

THE BASICS

2. Position the center punch on the marked point. As shown in the photo, hit the top of the center punch with the chasing hammer to slightly indent, or

dimple, the silver. (This dimple guides the drill bit so it rests where you intend to pierce the silver, rather than perilously sliding around the metal surface, making marks and putting you and your tools at risk.)

3. Place the dimpled silver on a block of scrap wood. This block supports the silver and protects the drill bit from being damaged after it passes through the metal.

4. Securely install a drill bit into the flexible shaft (see photo). I recommend using a bit with a 1-mm diameter. This size is large enough to produce a hole that is clearly visible and easy to work with. 1-mm bits are also inexpensive and simple to replace.

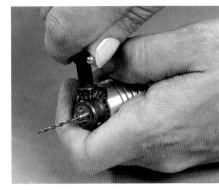

5. Firmly hold the flexible shaft at a 90-degree angle to the silver. Drill through the sheet at the dimpled mark (see photo).

Dimpled silver

Sawing Pierced Silver

Once you drill a hole in a sterling silver sheet, you can create an interior cutout form.

1. Loosen the nut at the bottom of the saw frame and free the blade (see photo). Leave the nut at the top of the frame secure, tightly holding the upper end of the saw blade.

2. Thread the free end of the blade through the hole drilled in the silver, making sure any transferred or marked design is visible from the top of the saw frame.

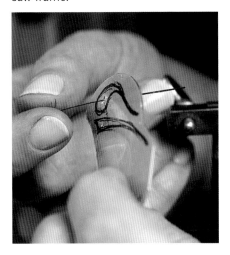

3. Slide the silver to the top of the saw blade as far as possible for support. Compress the saw frame between your jeweler's bench or work surface and your sternum. As shown in the photo, reattach the saw blade at the bottom of the frame, and tighten the bottom nut. The saw blade is now positioned to cut from within the sheet metal.

4. Use full and proper saw strokes to completely cut out the lines of the interior pattern.

5. Once the interior sawing is complete, slide the metal up the blade to the top of the frame. Compress the frame, and loosen the lower nut to release the bottom end of the blade. As shown in the photo, slide the metal down and off the blade. Repeat this process for each area you need to cut out.

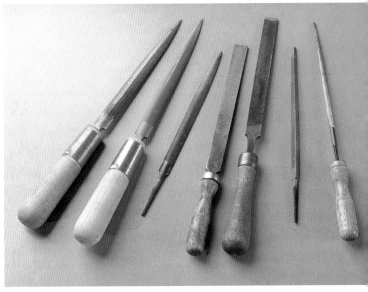

Files: coarse, medium, and fine

Filing & Sanding Silver

Though perhaps not as glamorous as other silversmithing techniques, filing and sanding are vital to every silver project. Without them, silver could not be cleaned and smoothed to its fullest potential.

Files

Files come in handy all the time for tasks such as cleaning, trimming, and shaping. The half-round file is the most versatile shape. It's important to have coarse, medium, and fine files in your studio at all times.

Needle Files

A cut or pierced piece of sterling silver has rough edges and unattractive saw marks. You can remove all the burrs and blemishes of cut metal with needle files, an essential cleaning tool for any silversmith. Needle files are small, and many of them end in a needle-like point. Often sold in sets, they come in different shapes and sizes and with different tooth. Some needle files are coarse, perfect for cleaning up a mess, while others are extra fine for delicate finishing. Most hardware stores sell basic needle file sets in medium to coarse cuts. These will work well for silversmithing projects. Common needle file shapes include round, oval, triangle, flat, two-sided flat, and one-sided flat. Since you'll need to file metal almost every time you make a cut, always keep a set of needle files somewhere convenient.

Needle File Shape	Recommended Application
oval, half-round, or round	curves and circles
flat	straight lines or sweeping around the outside of a curve
diamond or angled flat	corners and angles

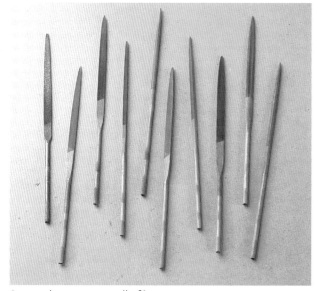

Assorted common needle files

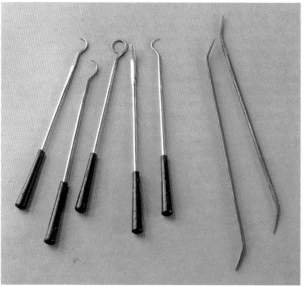

Assorted specialty needle files

Using Needle Files

Needle files only work in one direction. They remove metal on the forward stroke. If you exert pressure on both the forward and backward strokes, you'll clog the file, and since needle files don't clean easily or well, you'll shorten its life. If you find it easier to keep the file resting on the metal on the backward stroke, then do so without applying pressure.

Using a needle file inside a pierced and cutout design

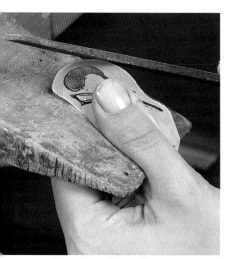

Using a forward stroke to file a cut silver edge

Sandpaper, Emery Cloth & Crocus Paper

These abrasive papers are useful for creating uniform surfaces, flattening bases, and removing firescale. Always use moist wet/dry sandpapers on metal. The grit on common brown sandpaper isn't affixed well enough to use on metal. Moistening the paper helps protect your lungs by suppressing the amount of particulates in the air. Keep in mind that the higher the sandpaper is numbered, the finer its grit. Crocus paper has a more meticulously measured grit than sandpaper or emery cloth. Crocus paper lasts moderately longer than sandpaper, and generally costs more.

Rubbing silver across sandpaper to smooth and level its edge

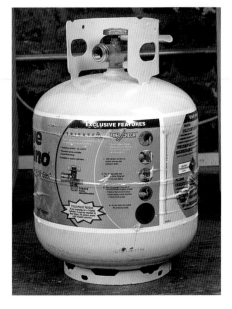

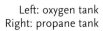

Heating Silver

During the process of creating a silver piece, you'll often anneal the metal to loosen its molecular structure. You'll also use heat to solder silver.

Torches

A torch is the most common and convenient way to achieve high temperatures in controlled areas. To create most silversmithing projects, you'll need to use one, and it's easier than you may think. Depending upon the type of gas they use as fuel, torches may be classified either as oxy-acetylene or oxy-propane. I prefer to use an oxy-propane torch. Propane burns cleaner and is easier to obtain. In order to burn whichever gas you choose, you'll need a supply of air or oxygen. Air is fine, compressed air is better, but my favorite by far is pure oxygen because it burns hotter.

THE BASICS

Fully assembled propane torch

Purchasing Torch Supplies

You can locate a local welding supplier in the telephone book. They sell oxygen and air tanks, dual gauge regulators, hoses, and LP gauges. How about that for handy one-stop shopping?

Oxygen or Air Tanks

It's much smarter and more economical to buy your first oxygen or air tank from your local welding supplier. After buying your first tank, all future purchases become less expensive because you simply trade in your empty tank for a full one. If you choose to buy a new tank, it will be shipped to you empty. When you go to have it "filled," most welding suppliers will just swap your new tank for a full used one.

Propane Tanks

Propane tanks have become incredibly popular and are frequently used for outdoor cooking. They're manufactured in three standard sizes. The smallest variety is disposable. Medium-size propane tanks are the most common for grilling and barbecues. Larger tanks are made for grills or for camping and recreational vehicles.

The small tanks hold less propane, must be disposed of when empty, and, in the long run, aren't particularly economical. They may not hold enough fuel to generate the amount of fire silversmiths need on a regular basis.

The medium-size tank is the most convenient for silversmithing. You can purchase one at any home improvement center or hardware store. These tanks are equipped with threaded openings so you can easily install the gauge regulators. If you have any concerns, take the regulator with you when you purchase your propane tank, and have the salesperson double-check to make sure you have the correct connection threads. Once you use up the propane gas, simply take the tank back and swap it out for another one, filled and ready to go. I keep two medium tanks hooked up in my studio, one to each torch. I also keep a spare tank in case I run out of propane at an inconvenient time. (With an extra tank, I can also become a barbecue hero!)

Regulators, Torch Heads & Nibs

An LP dual regulator will fit a medium-size propane tank without any problems or modifications. Using one is super simple and clean, and I have more than one torch set up this way. The torch head has two knobs, one to control the gas and one to control the air or oxygen. Since there are different gauges and different torch heads for the different gas types, it's important for you to talk to your local welding supplier and make sure you purchase the correct accessories for the type of gas you're using. Also make sure your torch head comes with *nibs*, the attachments on the tip of the torch controlling the size of the flame.

Controlling Fuel with Dual-Gauge Regulators

To heat metal you'll need to control the two sources of fuel (propane and air or oxygen) so they combine properly and are served to you at the correct pressure. Dual-gauge regulators will perform this task. Having two gauges permits the regulator to do two things. The gauge closest to the tank tells you how much fuel is in the tank. The second gauge, the one farther from the tank, tells you at how much pressure the fuel is being served. You'll attach these gauges to color-coded hoses to make things easier. A green hose is for the oxygen or air, and a red hose is for the gas. These hoses line up, connect to each other, and then are capped with screws that you attach to the torch head.

17

THE BASICS

Torch heads, nibs

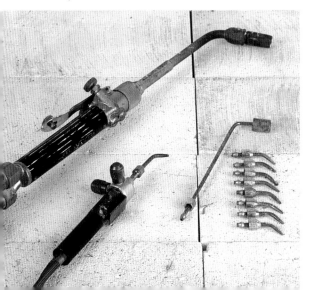

Dual-gauge regulators

Setting Up a Torch with Propane

1. Make certain that both the fuel tanks are in the OFF position. (They should have been sold to you this way.) Attach the dual-gauge regulators to the tanks, and tighten them with a wrench (see photo). Remember, red regulator or gauge to the propane tank, and green regulator or gauge to the oxygen or air tank. Angle the regulator dials up so you can see them.

2. Attach the hoses to the regulators—red to propane, green to oxygen or air. Use a wrench to tighten this connection (see photo).

3. Attach the hose ends to the torch—red to red, green to green (see photo). Make sure the torch knobs are both turned to the OFF position—right for tight, or clockwise.

4. There is a threaded dial in the middle of the fuel gauge to control the diaphragm. Turn the dial counter-clockwise to loosen it and open the regulator (see photo). The torch and tank are still in the OFF position, so it won't let fuel out, and the diaphragm of the regulator is open. This makes the regulator last longer. (If the diaphragm is already set when you open the tanks, it will get damaged.)

Turning on a Propane Torch

1. Open both fuel tank knobs as shown in the photo. This doesn't have to be a simultaneous action; just open them both. The pressure gauge closest to the tanks will jump, indicating you have fuel.

2. Keeping your eye on the second gauge, the one farther from the tank and closer to the hose, tighten the threaded dial with clockwise turns (see photo). The needle inside the second gauge will start to climb, displaying the PSI level. (PSI is an abbreviation for *pounds per square inch*, the standard measurement for pres-

sure.) Set the gauges for 10 pounds of pressure. This is the most pressure you'll ever need for an oxy-propane torch. (Oxyacetylene and other gas mixtures may require different pressures. Always ask your welding supplier for his or her suggestions. Make sure they know you're not setting up a cutting torch.)

3. Check the striker to make sure it sparks. Slightly twist the propane knob to open the flow to the torch. You shouldn't hear or see the gas. If you do, you have opened the knob too far. Position the striker in front of the nose of the torch, and strike it until a flame ignites (see photo page 19, top left). Because

Annealing a fluxed silver sheet

it hasn't been fed its air or oxygen, the flame will come from the nib of the torch and curve up. Put down the striker.

4. Gently open the oxygen or air knob. If the flame from the torch is too weak, the oxygen will blow out the gas; if the flame is too strong, the oxygen or air will make the flame even larger. Getting the flame just right takes practice.

Applying flux to a silver sheet

Annealing Silver

Annealing is an important part of creating a silver piece. This process may often interrupt the flow of your work, but don't fight it. Just stop what you're doing (usually hammering), take the silver to your soldering station, and re-anneal it. If you don't regularly loosen the silver molecules with heat, the metal can become damaged and your hard work can become torn—not a particularly fun option. Frequent re-annealing saves you a lot of work and heartache in the long run.

Every hammer stroke work-hardens silver. Here are two distinct clues that tell you when to re-anneal.

• When the metal seems unwilling to move and starts to "fight" back
• When the sound of the hammering becomes high-pitched and tinny

There are tricks to annealing that make it an easier technique. The best, most common, and simplest to understand is applying a material to the silver surface called *flux*. Flux is a borax acid compound that helps keep oxygen away from metal, leaving it clean and free of contaminants. Flux is sold in paste and liquid form, and both varieties act and react similarly. I recommend silversmiths use paste flux because it more effectively covers large areas. Always avoid getting flux on you or in you as you work. Refer to page 31 for more information about flux.

Cleaning Heated Silver

Whether annealing or soldering, after you heat a silver surface with the torch in any way, you must immediately clean it in a pickle bath.

Pickle

Pickle is a super cleaning agent that works on nonferrous metals. It's an acid bath, usually sulfuric acid, that you can purchase from a jewelry supply store. Sulfuric acid works best warm, so pickling silver in a slower cooker is ideal. Pickle cleans the silver surface after annealing and soldering, and it purifies the metal between steps. The acid removes all of

Pickle (commonly sulfuric acid)

the leftover flux and any copper oxide that may have formed on the silver surface during heating. (Leftover flux impedes your work. It gets really messy and damages your tools. The presence of oxides can prevent you from soldering because solder won't flow on a dirty surface.)

Pickle produces a cleaner and more uniform silver surface to view. The better you can see your work, the better your work will be. Pickling removes the cop-

Clockwise from left: copper tongs, slow cooker, quench bucket

per from the surface structure, leaving a fine silver or pure silver outer layer. This layer isn't thick, but it does change how the silver looks when heated, making it easier for you to judge the temperature

> ### STERLING WORDS
>
> SILVER IS READY TO COME OUT OF A PICKLE BATH AFTER ABOUT 10 MINUTES. IT LOOKS COMPLETELY DIFFERENT. ITS SURFACE IS MATTE WHITE. THIS MEANS THAT THE PICKLE HAS DONE ITS JOB. IF THERE ARE ANY BITS THAT LOOK LIKE GLASS LEFT ON THE SILVER, PUT IT BACK IN THE PICKLE.

Top: placing annealed silver into a pickle bath
Bottom: removing clean silver from a pickle bath

of the metal. Your eyes won't be tricked by watching the copper react to the air. Instead, you'll see the silver reacting to the heat.

If you want to work with milder chemicals, you can substitute alum or citric acid. These pickle alternatives are often sold at pharmacies. All pickling agents need to be neutralized after they're used. You can dilute alum and citric acid, and then pour it down a sink with baking soda and running water. Sulfuric acid must first be neutralized with baking soda before it can be disposed of in a sink with running water. All of these chemicals will damage your tools if they aren't washed off the silver after pickling is complete. To make your tools last, always rinse and dry the silver before proceeding to a new step.

Copper Tongs

You'll need a pair of tongs to remove sterling silver pieces from a pickle bath. Different from tweezers, tongs are much longer and made of copper. It's important to use copper tongs with pickle because no ferrous materials can go in an acid bath without causing contamination. A contaminated pickle bath produces a copper-plate finish on silver which is difficult to remove.

Firescale

Firescale is an oxide formed in the top layer of silver as a reaction to heat and oxygen. This reaction leaves discolored reddish grey marks in the metal that become more noticeable over time. Flux helps to reduce firescale because it can prevent the surface of the metal from exposure to oxygen, but flux doesn't always stay on the silver. There are some new types of silver being introduced that are manufactured to reduce or eliminate firescale, but, as of yet, I haven't found one I like as much as traditional sterling silver.

Many people have a difficult time spotting firescale. Fortunately, there's a trick for detecting it. Simply hold a piece of tissue or tracing paper over a silver surface and see if any discolored areas seem to appear more clearly through it.

Firescale can only be eliminated by removing the surface of the metal. Tripoli polishing compound, sandpaper, crocus paper, files, or any other subtractive tool will remove it. You may not think of removing it, you may not care to remove it, but if you remove only part of the firescale on a piece, its presence becomes even more obvious over time than if you leave it alone. It's best to just use a polishing machine and get rid of the scale.

> ### STERLING WORDS
>
> WITH EXPERIENCE, YOU CAN SPOT FIRESCALE BY HOLDING A PIECE OF SILVER IN THE LIGHT AND ROCKING IT BACK AND FORTH.

ON A DIFFICULT DAY, ALL I HAVE TO DO IS LOOK AT MY HAMMERS AND I START TO FEEL BETTER.

Organizing hammers and stakes in a wooden storage station

Hammering Silver

Hammers are what makes a smith a smith. I love them and could perhaps write an entire book about them. Hammers are prized possessions in silversmithing studios. They aren't the rusty ball-peen hammers found in junk drawers. They're the tools that define what you do, what you can do, and what you will do.

Mirror hammer face (top), marred hammer face (bottom)

Hammer Care

You need to take care of your hammers for them to function at their highest level. It's best to store hammers in a cool dry place. If you don't have an area with good climate control, think of some other way to keep them clean and their surface true. Ideally, I like to keep my hammers wrapped in cotton, leather, or flannel sleeves hanging on shelves inside a cabinet with a dehumidifier. This storage system allows me to spend less time resurfacing hammers, and more time actually using them! It doesn't take long for scars and pits to deface your tools, and these problems are very obvious because the original tool surfaces are so pristine.

Stakes and hammers are steel, not stainless steel. If you don't treat them with special care they become defaced, and, in turn, they deface the silver surface. Any pits or marks on the faces of hammers and stakes transfer onto the silver. The best way to handle this situation is to prevent pits from happening at all, or for as long as you can. Otherwise, you'll have to clean your silver pieces even more than normal to remove scars left by tools. Here are three ways to prolong a good surface on your hammers and stakes.

• Rinse all of the pickle off the silver before working with stakes and hammers. Acid can mark and mar tools, even if it's dry. Air is never completely dry, so any leftover acid could transfer to your tools.

• Thoroughly dry your silver. If you don't, you expose your tools to oxidation and rust that can cause damage.

• Keep your hammering area clean. Driven by the force of a hammer blow, even dust and polishing compounds can pit hammers and stakes.

21

THE BASICS

Hammer Types

There are countless types of hammers. Many silversmiths transform their hammers over the years, customizing them for specific tasks. Some smiths I know scour antique malls or used tool stores for new (to them!) hammers to add to their collections. Beginning silversmiths need only a few common types. Two of the most important are a good planishing hammer and a rawhide, wooden, or rubber mallet.

Planishing Hammer

Every time you use a planishing hammer, you'll change the surface of the silver through movement and hardening. You may be creating new marks or replacing large marks with smaller, more controlled ones. You already know that silver hardens as its molecules get pushed closer together. This happens even faster when you hammer metal *with* metal (and even faster when you hammer metal with metal on top of a metal surface!).

You can buy a planishing hammer from any jewelry supply store. This type of hammer has two faces, one slightly domed and the other one flatter. Both faces should have a clean and bright mirror surface. This is important because everything you hit with the planishing hammer will show its surface. Since the hammer surface is the impression left on the silver, you want it to be immaculate. A blow with a clean hammer produces a clean surface; whereas a blow with a

Planishing hammers

Rawhide mallets

pitted hammer leaves unwanted marks on the metal. To preserve its mirror finish, use a planishing hammer only on the surface of nonferrous metals and never use it for any other odd jobs.

Making Your Own Planishing Hammer
If you don't want to purchase a planishing hammer, you can make one out of a ball-peen hammer. This process takes time and an eye for detail, but it will work. A homemade planishing hammer won't have the balance of a commercial one, but it's satisfactory for beginning silversmiths.

1. Use a rough-grit belt sander to grind down the flat face of the ball-peen hammer until it's completely smooth.

2. File the edges of the flat hammer face into a gentle curve. (Only file the edges; you don't want to leave marks on the face.)

3. Use sandpaper to polish the face of the hammer (see photo). Gradually downgrade the paper's grit until you achieve a mirror finish. Leave the edges of the hammer softly curved.

Sinking hammers

Chasing hammers

Forging hammers

Rawhide, Wooden & Rubber Mallets

Mallets don't exert the same force as other silversmithing hammers, but they're invaluable for many tasks. You'll use a mallet when you don't want to alter the surface of the silver. I use a rawhide mallet, but a wooden or rubber mallet also will work well.

Sinking Hammer

Every silversmithing shop needs at least one sinking hammer. This useful tool is similar in size and weight to a planishing hammer, but it has domed and rounded mirror faces. You'll use a sinking hammer to force silver down, or "sink" it into a surface that's curved, cupped, domed, or stretched. In silversmithing terms, this process is called *sinking*. Other metalworkers may refer to it as *dishing*. Both terms are correct. Sinking uses a curved hammer to stretch silver down into a cavity and creates a greater surface area.

Ball-Peen Hammer

You'll use a ball-peen hammer to hit small metalworking tools. The face of a ball-peen hammer doesn't need a clean surface. You can even use one you

already have in your toolbox or lying around your home. Just remember, ball-peen hammers are only for hitting other tools, never silver.

Chasing Hammer

For hammering other tools with great control, the small and light chasing hammer is unsurpassed. A chasing hammer looks like a ball-peen hammer with a wider, horizontal flat face. It's smaller and oblong on the opposite, rounded face. It has a narrow neck that usually flares out at the grip for a good hold. Chasing hammers are manufactured in various weights and always come with a mirror finish on the flat face. This pristine surface will quickly become marred, pitted, grooved, and scratched—and this is a good thing! A chasing hammer is one of the only tools for which a distressed surface is desirable. It helps prevent the hammer from sliding off the tool that's being struck.

Forging Hammer

A forging hammer is for pushing and moving silver. It usually has two ends that each taper to V. A forging hammer leaves a horizontal mark whenever and wher-

ever it's used. Its force moves metal in opposite directions to the horizontal blow. Like the planishing hammer, one end of the forging hammer is a bit more curved than the other. This is important to remember, so you know how much of the surface area you're hitting at one time, and so you gain maximum control over your materials. A forging hammer doesn't need a mirror surface, but its face shouldn't be excessively disfigured. You don't want to mar the metal more than necessary upon contact. If a forging hammer develops enough tooth to actually cut through metal, it needs to be cleaned and resurfaced immediately.

Using a forging hammer on silver always leaves horizontal marks

Hammering station with wooden table

Hammering table at the correct height for me

Setting Up a Hammer Station

A hammer station is a dedicated area where a silversmith is best set up to hammer. Different hammering skills are performed better at different heights, so an ideal hammer station would be able to accommodate all of them.

Many silversmiths acquire and customize tree stumps to suit their needs. A tree trunk can have several depressions cut into it to use as sinking areas. Depending upon the individual's needs, these depressions can have various depths and diameters. Other areas of the trunk could have square craters cut out to hold various stakes and other hammering surfaces. Not all stakes have the same size base, so multiple trunk holes would be needed. (If you have one stake you use more than the rest, you can permanently mount it, and leave other cavities free to hold other stakes and tools.)

If you don't want to use a tree trunk, you can make a hammer station out of wood. It must be a very sturdy and sound structure to bear the brunt of the considerable force you'll be exerting upon and through it. I recommend using a solid piece of wood, about 1½ inches (3.8 cm) thick, for the top of the station. (A heavy door would work well.) Mount it on legs made of 4 x 4 lumber. The total height of the station, including its top surface, should be no more than 3 feet (.9 m). A good way to judge the correct height for your station is to build it as

Large vise attached to a hammering table

high as your wrist when your arm is hanging at your side. (This is also the approximate height of your thigh/pelvis joint.) Once the hammering tools are attached to the station, their working surfaces will be level with the height of your elbow. This is the correct position for many silversmithing tools and techniques, but not all. You may want to build an alternative lower surface, or, like many silversmiths who use the tree trunk, build a very low surface and sit down to work. You can then adjust your height by changing your chair. Frame the station all the way around, including at least two cross-angle supports. One of the most helpful accessories you can add to a hammer station is a large vise. I have a 45-pound (21.4 kg) vise on my table, and it comes in handy all the time.

Hammering Surfaces

Silversmiths need a variety of hardened steel surfaces on which to hammer their work. Swage blocks, anvils, and stakes reliably perform this important function.

Swage Block or Anvil

A swage block or an anvil is a required tool for almost every silversmithing project. You can use either one, based on availability and your comfort. Whichever steel surface you select should be clean and without bumps or pits. (Similar to the planishing hammer, any defects on the swage block or anvil

Swage block

will show up on your silver.) A swage block is a large steel block with different faces. One face should be flat, but others can have indentations, channels, and curves. You can purchase a swage block from a supply house that caters to *farriers*, or horseshoe makers. You'll be relieved to know that you don't need to find and buy an actual anvil. (These days they can be very hard to locate and very expensive!) One alternative to purchas-

ing a swage block or anvil would be to use a railroad tie. Clean and polish its surface using the same procedure described in "Making Your Own Planishing Hammer" on page 22. A railroad tie doesn't need a genuine mirror finish; a good steel wool finish from a rotary sander will be sufficient.

From left: carved stake cavity, stake adapter, commercial stake cavity

Stakes

Stakes are hammering surfaces shaped specifically for certain silversmithing tasks. They can be made of various materials, such as wood and rigid plastic, but the most common stakes are made of tooled steel. Along with hammer-hunting, finding interesting stakes can also be a silversmith's obsession. You can purchase a small variety of stakes through jewelry supply stores. I buy them whenever and wherever I can find them. Once you learn about stakes and see a few versions, then you can scour your local used hardware stores for ones to add to your supply. Anywhere you run across an

antique anvil, you're likely to find some fantastic old stakes. With some major cleaning, a crummy-looking old stake can be an indispensable new smithing tool. (Another wonderful thing about reclaiming old stakes is that they're usually affordable. Most people either don't have a use for them or don't know what they are.) Stakes are available in several basic shapes, and their shapes are pretty true to their names. There are also adapters that allow you to set up stakes at different heights or in different size cavities on a hammering station.

STERLING WORDS

An anvil is a great find. If you see one for sale you think you can clean, buy it—or let me know about it!

Mushroom stakes

T-stakes

Mushroom Stakes

A mushroom stake is usually the first type of stake new silversmiths acquire. It is a very useful and versatile tool. You'll use this stake to support the inside of a curved silver object as you planish and refine the outside. The base of the mushroom stake fits into a hole in a hammer station or into an anvil cavity. The top of the stake is always the hammering surface. Mushroom stakes balloon outward near the top, where they're fabricated into a variety of shapes. The "mushroom" dome can have a large or small diameter, and it can be tall or even flat.

Planishing on a mushroom stake

T-Stakes

The base of the T-stake fits into a hammer station hole or anvil cavity. The top of the stake branches out in two directions, similar to the letter "T." The branches aren't identical on both sides. Usually, a different hammering surface is offered on either end of the T. (Some stakes even offer a third hammering surface on the area just above the base support.) T-stakes vary tremendously (and wonderfully) in form. Horn stakes are part of this tool "family." One end of a horn stake curves around, and its other end is long and tapered like a ring mandrel.

Hammering on a T-stake

Additional Stakes

There are some small stakes designed and fabricated just for shaping. Spoon stakes, available in a variety of sizes, allow you to create uniform spoon faces. There are doming stakes, edging stakes, flaring stakes, cutting stakes, punching stakes, bottoming stakes, silversmith stakes, cup stakes, fluting stakes, molding stakes—and the list goes on and on. I, of course, want one of each, but even though I've been silversmithing for years, I still only have a small collection. This goes to show that you don't need all of the stakes on the market, or even many of them, to make great work. Simply get your hands on the most versatile, a few mushroom stakes and a few T-stakes, and get started!

Assorted additional stakes

Dapping blocks

Dapping Tools

A dapping tool, or dap, is a small tool, usually handheld, that has a rounded face like a sinking hammer. Dapping tools are often sold in sets of various sizes. Because they're very handy, I recommend purchasing a set, but you can also make your own.

Dapping tools

Making a Dapping Tool
WHAT YOU NEED

Steel dowel, 5 inches (12.7 cm) long, diameter to fit dapping block

Metal cleanser (optional, if steel dowel is rusty)

Electric belt sander

Sandpapers for belt sander, coarse and fine

Sandpaper, coarse and fine

Black aluminum oxide

Flexible shaft or polishing lathe with stiff buffing wheel

WHAT YOU DO

1. Clean the surface of the steel dowel with the metal cleanser as needed to remove rust. As shown in the photo, use the electric belt sander with the coarse sandpaper to grind down and round one end of the steel dowel. Change to a finer sandpaper, and use the belt sander to clean the ground dowel end.

2. Sand the surface of the ground and cleaned dowel by hand, progressing from coarse to fine grits of paper.

3. Use the black aluminum oxide on a stiff buffing wheel attached to the flexible shaft or the polishing lathe to give the dowel its final clean and shine.

Dapping Blocks

A dapping block is a block with one or more semicircular or domed cavities. Dapping blocks are available in different sizes, often sold with matching daps that fit into the block's indentations, and frequently made of steel. Depending on the size of the dap and block, these tools can be perfect for making silver beads or as a way to start sinking. You can use a sandbag or a carved wooden block instead of an actual dapping block, but having the real thing will make your work much easier and faster. If you want to make your own, start with a good piece of hardwood. Drill out cavities of the desired sizes and depths, and then chisel the drilled holes to form rounder indentations. A sandbag or a custom-carved block is preferable to a commercial dapping block when you need an irregular-size or custom indentation.

Hammering into a dapping block

Sandbag

Left: planished silver surface
Right: mirror silver surface

Sandbag

A sandbag is another useful tool, especially if you don't have a dapping block. Sandbags yield just enough to allow silver to move, while also having sufficient stability to support the areas not being hammered. This balance allows the proper stretching to occur. A sandbag is not as efficient as a dapping block, but some silversmiths love them for the control and flexibility they offer. You can construct one out of thick canvas and fill it with sand or sawdust, or you can purchase a sandbag at any jewelry supply house or home improvement center.

Hammering into a sandbag

Different Silver Surfaces—
Planished & Mirror

Silversmiths traditionally planish to *remove* hammer marks from silver, but if the metal is smooth to begin with, planishing creates a nice, shiny, hammered texture. A planished silver surface is distinguished by many small stacked rows of hammer marks made with a mirror-surfaced hammer. A planished finish requires less cleaning. Silver with a mirror surface is completely smooth and highly polished.

Planishing Silver

Planishing flat sheet metal is a good way to develop your eye-hand coordination for smithing. With practice, you'll develop a feel for where the hammer is landing in relation to the metal.

1. Place a piece of sterling silver sheet metal on top of a swage block or anvil.

2. Using the slightly domed face of the planishing hammer,* hit the silver at the point where it's in contact with the swage block or anvil (see photo). The silver will move and curve upward.

3. Continue to hammer the silver in straight rows, making sure the hammer is hitting the metal where it touches the block or anvil. With practice, your hammer blows will become more uniform, leaving a beautiful surface on the silver.

Although the flatter face of the planishing hammer leaves less noticeable marks on silver, the marks its edges make are more pronounced, especially for beginning silversmiths. The flatter face of the planishing hammer is more useful for hammering the outside of a domed surface.

METAL NEEDS ANNEALING BETWEEN HAMMERING "TURNS." IT CAN'T KEEP TAKING THE HAMMER BLOWS AND REMAIN FLEXIBLE. METAL THAT'S NOT ANNEALED BETWEEN TURNS GETS STIFFER, HARDER, AND MORE BRITTLE. EVENTUALLY IT WILL SHATTER. THIS IS KIND OF NEAT TO SEE, BUT PROBABLY ISN'T THE CONDITION YOU INTEND TO ACHIEVE.

Sinking & Raising

Raising and sinking both give metal volume, but they change and manipulate the metal in completely different ways.

Sinking stretches silver down. It doesn't increase the actual amount of metal. By hammering into a depression or a sandbag, the areas being hit are being stretched, and volume is being created. This makes the hammered areas thinner, but not so thin that the integrity of the metal is compromised.

Raising is the opposite of sinking, though visually the two processes create very similar results. Raising is hammering silver on a stake, pushing it in on itself, and, in effect, thickening it. Raising brings up the sides; sinking pushes down the bottom.

This is an important difference. For example, if you sink a silver disk with a 7-inch (17.8 cm) diameter, the diameter of the resulting bowl would still be close to 7 inches (17.8 cm). If you raise the same disk, its diameter would decrease as its sides were brought up and in. A raised bowl could be just as deep; it could even hold the same volume, but the diameter of its opening would be transformed drastically.

Below: three stages of sinking a silver disk

Below: raising a silver disk

Marking Circular Guidelines on Three-Dimensional Silver Forms

As a silversmith, you'll often have to draw hammering guidelines on three-dimensional silver forms that have some vertical volume. This is particularly relevant when you sink and raise silver. Here is a very simple way to form these helpful guidelines.

1. Make a small hole on the side edge of your work surface.

2. Place one part of a compass or divider in this hole. The other end of the tool will stick up above your work surface.

3. Adjust the compass or divider to the measurement you need. Tighten the tool in this position.

4. Rotate the three-dimensional silver piece against the free compass or divider end, and mark the circular guidelines. For added accuracy, place the silver piece on a lazy Susan before rotating it against the compass or divider.

Physical Fitness & Hammering Safety

Some advanced silversmithing projects require major amounts of hammering. These pieces require so much physical effort that they cannot safely be completed in a day or even two. I bring this up because safety is important to all silversmiths, and hammering is a major part of our craft. Safety needs to include physical maintenance. Make sure you're comfortable at your hammer station. If a stake sits too high on your station, either make a lower station or a pedestal on which to stand. (I recommend keeping a pedestal in your studio. Gaining additional height can be an advantage for some tasks.)

Allow your body time to rest and heal during long periods of hammering. If you're not accustomed to heavy physical work, you should stop and rest anytime your body aches. If you are accustomed to intense labor, you should still rest your arms and body at least every 20 minutes. Stop hammering after a certain period of time, and walk, rest, sit, chat, whatever. This break should equal the time spent hammering. Silversmithing is not a test of will or a contest. It isn't something that you should stress over, either mentally or physically. It's simply a fun activity you should enjoy, so take your time and always be mindful of your body.

STERLING WORDS

SOLDERING SOUNDS TERRIBLY COMPLICATED, BUT YOU ONLY NEED THREE THINGS—HEAT, FLUX, AND SOLDER. EVERYTHING ELSE COMES WITH PRACTICE.

Soldering Silver

Silversmiths solder to join together metal. This process uses a metal alloy with a lower melting temperature (solder) to bond silver pieces.

Butt soldering two silver pieces

Soldering Methods

Butt-soldering and sweat-soldering are the two major methods. A butt-solder is made when two metal edges are positioned next to each other, and flowing solder is run down their seam (see figure 1). A sweat-solder is made when two metal pieces are positioned on top of each other, and the solder is flowed between the sheets (see figure 2).

PIECE A   PIECE B

figure 1

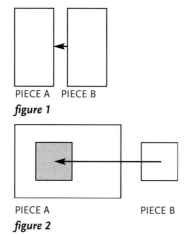

PIECE A   PIECE B

figure 2

Solder Types

There are many types of solder readily available from jewelry suppliers. The most common, and the one you'll be using in this book are three high-temperature solders: hard, medium, and easy. These solders are categorized by the *flow point*, the temperature at which the solder flows (usually between 1325° and 1450°F [718° and 788°C]). Hard solder has the hottest flow point, medium solder is in the middle, and easy solder has the lowest flow point. (All of these solders are now available without cadmium, a substance that lets out harmful gases and fumes when heated.) Hard solder has the highest silver content, medium solder contains less silver, and easy solder even less. This has great effect on your work. Not only does the solder silver content alter its flow temperature, but it also affects the color of the solder. Hard solder most closely resembles sterling silver. It will be the least visually disruptive, but it will flow at temperatures close to the melting point of silver, and may not be the best solder for every task. Easy solder is very yellow in color. It can dramatically interfere with the look of a silver piece if not well-planned and well-executed.

Hard solder, medium solder, easy solder

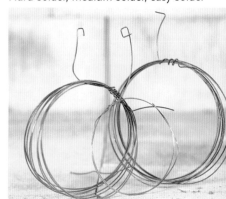

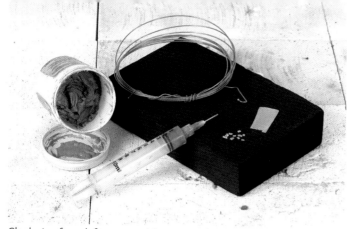

Clockwise from left: paste solder, wire solder, sheet solder, solder pallions, syringe for applying paste solder

Cutting sheet solder into pallions

Solder Forms

Solder is manufactured in several forms, such as sheet, wire, and paste. I prefer using wire solder, but each silversmith has her own favorite. When I work with wire solder, especially on large silver pieces, I'm comfortable holding the torch in one hand and the wire in the other. People who use sheet solder like it because they can cut it into tiny chips, or *pallions*, and place it directly where needed.

Characteristics of Solder

• *Solder always flows toward the heat.* If you unevenly heat the silver, the solder will "jump," not staying where you intended it to run. For example, if you're butt-soldering a joint and you heat one side of the seam more than the other, the solder will "jump" onto the hotter side and never connect the two silver pieces.
• *Solder will never fill in gaps.* All edges you intend to solder must be in contact in order for the solder to flow. If there are gaps between the silver pieces or uneven contact, the solder won't flow.
• *Solder will properly flow only on a clean silver surface.*
• *Solder pits when it's overmelted.* Pits are tiny holes which cause soldered seams to be even more visible. As your soldering skills improve and you achieve more control, pitting will become less of a problem.

Caring for Solder

Carefully mark the different types of solder you use so you won't get them confused. If you use hard solder for one seam and want to switch to medium solder for the next seam, you need to know which solder is which. Once you use a medium solder, you don't want to accidently reach for the hard solder, and heat up the silver to the temperature at which hard solder flows. This would melt all of the medium solder seams.

Soldering Tools & Materials

Many of the tools and materials you use to anneal silver also are used to solder it, such as a torch, flux, and a pickle bath.

Flux

Flux is a borax acid mixture that prevents oxygen from reaching the silver surface. You must use flux when soldering. The oxygen in the air and in the torch reacts with the silver to form an oxide layer where you want to heat the metal. Solder won't flow on this or any dirty surface. Flux forms a barrier between the oxygen and the metal, allowing the metal to get hot without the oxide forming, and keeping the metal clean enough for the solder to flow. Flux also helps prevent *firescale*, the oxidation of silver beneath its surface. Flux doesn't eliminate firescale, but it does retard its appearance.

You can purchase flux in dry cone form and grind it with alcohol to create a paste. A more common and popular option is to buy pre-mixed flux in paste or liquid form. Paste flux is applied to cool silver with a brush. Liquid flux can be poured into a spray bottle and sprayed on cool silver. With practice, you can spray liquid flux on hot metal, too. I use both paste and liquid flux.

Once you flux the silver surface, use an oxy-propane torch to dry it. The flux will first turn white, then start to bubble, and finally turn clear. As it turns clear the flux resembles a pasty sticky film on the metal. This indicates the metal has reached the correct annealing temperature. The clear film acts like molten glass, forming a thin layer on the metal surface and protecting it from contaminants.

Clockwise from left: paste flux, liquid flux, spray bottle with liquid flux, brushes for paste flux

Binding wire

I HAVE QUITE A TWEEZER COLLECTION, AND WHENEVER I SEE THEM ON SALE I BUY MORE. THEY AREN'T EXPENSIVE, AND YOU CERTAINLY DON'T NEED TO BUY THE FINEST OR MOST EXPENSIVE SET. YEARS AGO I BOUGHT MY FAVORITE SOLDERING TWEEZERS FROM A STREET VENDOR FOR SPARE CHANGE. THEY STILL WORK, AND I KEEP THEM CLEAN AND HANDY ALL THE TIME.

Binding Wire

When creating some projects you'll secure the silver at various stages with binding wire. Most commonly used when soldering, this wire can hold metal pieces in place, ensuring you solder where and when you want to. When silver is heated for soldering, the flux bubbles and can cause the metal to move, or the metal itself may shift due to heat expansion. Binding wire guards against excess motion. If you have an odd angle that requires support during soldering, binding wire often can handle the job.

Many jewelry suppliers sell binding wire in various gauges. I recommend using 18- to 20-gauge stainless steel wire. Thinner wire absorbs heat so quickly that it breaks easily. Thicker binding wire works better on larger pieces. Extra-thick binding wire can leave marks on the metal, and it's difficult to manipulate and secure. Because all binding wire will eventually be discarded, it doesn't need to be expensive or attractive to work.

You must remove all traces of binding wire from a soldered piece of silver before placing it into a pickle bath. Not all binding wire is made from stainless steel. If you accidentally get a ferrous metal, or even a chip of it, in the pickle bath, you could contaminate the pickle and copper-plate the soldered silver piece.

Tweezers

Silversmiths can never have too many pairs of tweezers, and they don't need to be pretty. They're going to get torched, discolored, and covered with solder and all sorts of other messy things. You don't need to spend lots of money on tweezers. Look in a tool catalog first to get a good idea of what types of tweezers are available, and then go to a discount hardware store and buy a multiple pack.

Using a torch makes metals hot. Tweezers are essential to use when you can't handle or manipulate the piece you're working on due to its heat. Standard tweezers are manufactured in many sizes and shapes. You'll want a long pair to use when you work for an extended period of time in a hot area. Long tweezers won't get too hot too fast. You'll want a small sharp set for precisely placing solder pallions on silver without moving or pushing it. Self-closing tweezers also come in many designs and can be very helpful. Some have heat stops on their handle, so that when you use them to hold two objects together in the flame, you'll be able to remove the tweezers without burning yourself.

Assorted tweezers (rear), wire clippers (front)

Self-closing tweezers

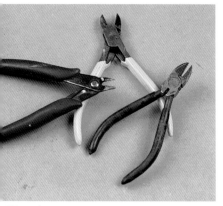
Wire clippers

Wire Clippers

You'll use wire clippers to cut solder into small pieces. Keep an extra pair at your solder station so they're always handy.

Setting Up a Soldering Station

In order to explore silversmithing, you need a place to solder, anneal, and do other heat-based work. I call this area the soldering station. (I have much of my studio set up in stations. This arrangement helps keep me, and my tools and materials organized.)

Creating a Heat-Resistant Environment

Surrounding your soldering station with heat-reflective materials will keep high temperatures away from your work surfaces. Firebricks repel heat well. You can purchase them from a ceramics supplier. A layer of firebricks prevents heat from reaching your table, your walls, or any of your work surfaces. It blocks these surfaces from being burned or scarred should a hot metal piece jump or roll during soldering or annealing. With this safety precaution in place, you won't need to worry if you're annealing a large silver piece and some of the heat from the torch misses the piece and travels out toward the wall. I strongly recommend setting up your soldering station with firebrick or some other fire-retardant and heat-reflective surface. Your local hardware store may carry other options.

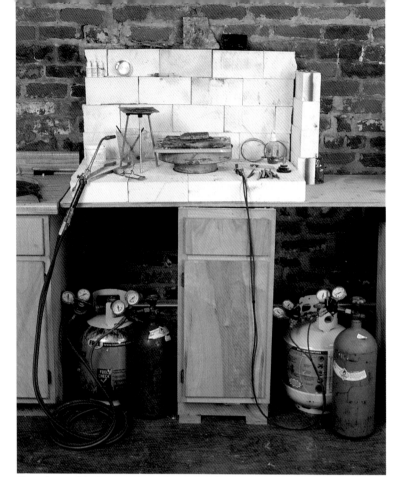
Complete soldering station with two torches

Heat-resistant firebricks

The photo above shows 3-inch-thick (7.6 cm) firebricks placed along the base and up the rear wall of a soldering station. The layer is 36 inches (.9 m) wide and climbs the wall approximately 30 inches (.7 m) high. Creating such a sizeable fire-resistant surface may be overkill for making jewelry or small projects, but when you start to anneal and work on large silver pieces, it's wise to err on the side of caution.

Ceramic plates

Soldering Surfaces

The firebrick layer is only a safety measure. You won't actually solder on top of the brick. It functions as a surface on which to place your soldering surfaces. Picture a chef in the kitchen. He or she doesn't cut food directly on the counter (the firebrick), but on a cutting board placed on top of the counter. There are several surfaces on which I enjoy soldering and that I can highly recommend. Putting one of these on top of the firebrick layer will provide you with a nice clean surface on which to solder and anneal, extend the life of the soldering station, and ensure that little or no heat will ever get through to your work surface.

Soldering Turntable

Similar to a lazy Susan, a soldering turntable rotates on a base. Its tray is filled with pumice stones on which silver is placed for soldering. A turntable allows you to rotate pieces as you work without touching them. Although not a necessity, a soldering turntable is great idea and extremely useful.

Soldering turntable with pumice stones

Ceramic Plate

When soldering, you can place a ceramic plate directly on top of the firebricks or on top of a turntable. The biggest drawback of soldering on a ceramic plate is that the plate absorbs heat. This means you may have to hold the torch to the silver longer than usual. Since the ceramic plate is a flat surface, however, it often provides better support than pumice stones. It's also a cleaner surface than pumice stones, producing little dust or other contaminants that interfere with soldering.

Honeycomb Ceramic Plate

Honeycomb ceramic plates are porous soldering surfaces. They cost more and will wear out faster than solid ceramic plates, but I love using them. They don't absorb as much heat as solid ceramics, and they provide a flat, dustless surface on which to solder.

Honeycomb ceramic plate

Charcoal Block

A charcoal block is a great tool to have on hand, but it's not as versatile as the two types of ceramic plates. It's a fantastic soldering surface for some applications, but not always good for others. A charcoal block absorbs heat, and sometimes this is desirable. A charcoal block is also soft. You can stick holding pins in it or carve it if needed. To use a charcoal block, you'll need to wrap some thick

Charcoal blocks

binding wire around its outer edge to hold it together. The binding wire prolongs the life of the block by helping to prevent its cracking. Leftover scraps of charcoal block can be very useful to prop up silver or hold it in place while you solder. (Very little gets thrown out in a silversmithing studio. It just gets used in different ways.)

Elevated tripod

Elevated Tripod

Elevated tripods are especially useful soldering surfaces. They allow you to position the torch under the piece of silver you're soldering and work from directions that otherwise would be inaccessible. A tripod usually has a center ring holding it together. A sheet of wire mesh rests on top of the tripod, and the silver piece you're soldering rests on top of the mesh. The wire mesh will burn, loose its integrity over time, and eventually need replacing, but the tripod base will last.

Soldering Station Safety

• Keep the fuel tank hoses away from the soldering station as much as possible. Tuck them under your work space if you can. You never want to set up your soldering station so you light a torch near the fuel hoses.

• Put a fire extinguisher in an accessible location. Make sure to check its numbers and codes to ensure it's the right type of extinguisher.

• Set up a vent hood or exhaust fan if you use a lot of flux or if you work in a space that isn't well ventilated. A standard kitchen range hood will draw away the solder and flux fumes. Some people set up their soldering stations near a window, in which case an exhaust fan would work.

Basic Soldering

WHAT YOU NEED

2 scrap sterling silver pieces, any gauge
Jeweler's saw and saw blades (optional)
Needle files (optional)
Wire clippers
Hard, medium, and easy solder (practice with each)
Flux, paste or liquid
Flux brush or spray bottle
Oxy-propane torch with striker
Tweezers
Pickle bath
Copper tongs

TECHNIQUES

Sawing (optional), page 12
Filing (optional), page 15

WHAT YOU DO

1. Line up the two scrap sterling silver pieces you want to solder (see photo). Make sure their edges are flush. Cut or file the edges as needed to secure a good fit.

2. Use the wire cutters to cut pallions of solder (see photo); set aside in a safe place.

3. Use the flux brush or spray bottle to apply paste or liquid flux to the sterling silver pieces.

4. Check the safety of the torch, and then light it with the striker.

5. Either put the solder pallions on the silver after the flux but before the heat, or apply them as you solder as shown in the photo. (If you put them on first, you may find the pallions moving as the flux heats up. Have a pair of tweezers ready to move the solder back on the seam so it flows in the proper place.)

6. Heat both silver surfaces until the flux turns clear and the annealing colors start to appear. Keep the torch moving at all times, but not too fast. Gently wave the torch over and around the seam of the silver, making sure to heat both sides and the entire length of the seam. The solder should ball up (see photo). This indicates it's about to flow.

7. Keep the heat gently moving, but concentrate on the seam. The solder will now flow into the seam as shown in the photo, joining the two silver pieces. If the seam is unevenly soldered, you can use the torch's heat to "pull" the solder where you want it to flow.

8. Cool the soldered silver. Place it in the pickle bath. Let it sit in the acid until the flux and oxides are removed. Use copper tongs to retrieve the soldered silver from the pickle bath. Thoroughly rinse and dry it.

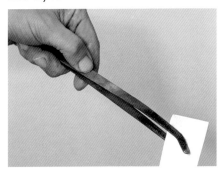

Tip: Prior to soldering you may need to work with awkward silver pieces to develop ways to make them sit properly and remain stable. One solution is to balance these pieces on a *third arm*, a jeweler's term for a set of tweezers held by its own armature and weight. You could also use a brick, some charcoal, or anything else that's fire-resistant and has enough weight and mass to hold the element in place.

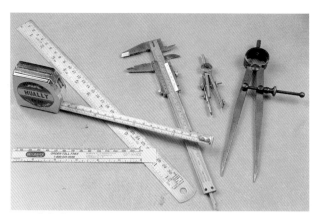

From left: flexible ruler, tape measure, metal ruler, calipers, small compass, large compass

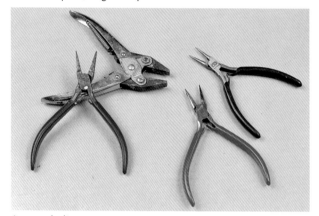

Assorted pliers

Clockwise from left: respirator, leather work apron, dust mask, safety glasses, work gloves

Essential Hand Tools & Supplies

The items described below don't belong to any particular station, but they're all indispensable silversmithing supplies.

Safety Gloves & Glasses

Safety is the first and foremost concern for any silversmith. You'll soon be working with fire and sharp (sometimes flying!) objects, so always take as many precautions as possible. Start by getting yourself a good pair of safety glasses and leather work gloves that fit well (neither snug nor bulky). You can buy both of these items at any hardware store.

Pliers

A silversmith's pliers are small. Flat-nose, needle-nose, and half-round pliers are all handy varieties. Some pliers are spring-mechanized to keep them open when not in use, while others are not. Like tweezers, pliers are sold in different shapes and sizes, are often sold in sets, and are available in a wide price range. My advice is to start at an affordable price range. If one pair of pliers breaks, buy another of a higher quality to replace it. Just remember that more expensive doesn't always mean higher quality!

Steel Dowels

Steel dowels are also referred to as *centers*, and you can buy them at any hardware store. They're manufactured in various diameters, from less than 1/8 inch (3 mm) to more than 2 inches (5 cm). Most dowels are approximately 6 to 8 inches (15.2 to 20.3 cm) long. It's a good idea to buy a whole set of steel dowels, as they'll frequently come in handy.

Wooden and steel dowels

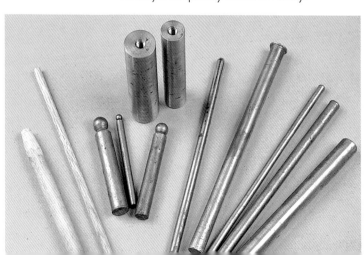

Tools & Techniques for Finishing Silver

Cleaning and polishing a silversmithed piece is just as important as forming one. To give your creations the shine they deserve, you must develop many new skills.

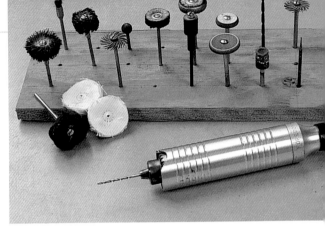

Flexible shaft with assorted attachments

Motorized Finishing Tools

The finishing tools you use will change and their numbers increase as your work and studio grow. If you're a beginning silversmith, you don't have to run out and buy a polishing lathe right away. Instead, you can use a smaller motorized rotary tool called a *flexible shaft* to finish your silver pieces. Its motor is separated from its hand piece by a long and flexible shaft, and it accepts a wide range of attachments, from drill bits and sanding disks to stitched cotton polishing wheels. Once you're committed to the craft of silversmithing, you might want to acquire a professional polishing lathe with an enclosed motor, a vent system, and a hood to reduce debris.

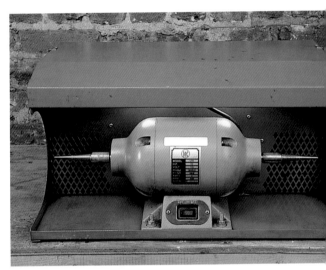

Polishing lathe

Polishing at the lathe wearing appropriate safety gear

Polishing Lathe

A polishing lathe is a large table-mounted tool with a one- or two-speed motor. Ideally, a beginning silversmith should have a 1/4-horsepower motor that runs at 1,725 revolutions per minute (rpm) at the very least. Attached to the lathe are arbors that hold polishing wheels. One arbor is sufficient, but a double-arbor setup will allow you to polish more efficiently.

Polishing on a lathe is dirty work. The machine should have a vent and a hood (a simple box attached to a vacuum will suffice). When working with a polishing lathe, you should always wear a dust mask and safety glasses and have a sink with running water and liquid soap nearby.

Polishing lathe arbor

Abrasive wheels for the polishing lathe

SAFETY FIRST

• *Polishing at the lathe is difficult and hazardous.* This can't be stressed often enough. You shouldn't work at the lathe if you're tired, if you don't feel well, or if you don't have on the appropriate safety gear.

• *Use caution when wearing work gloves.* You don't want a glove to get caught in the polishing lathe.

• *Don't buy a motor that's too powerful.* Any object that gets caught in the lathe will fly out of your control and hit something, such as the hood, the vent, or even you. This could damage your work or cause an injury. Use a single-phase light motor and be sure to exercise caution as you learn its power.

Abrasive Wheels

An abrasive wheel has more bite than any other polishing wheel. They come in many grades and grits. If you select one that's too abrasive, you could create more of a mess than you had to begin with. Abrasive wheels often have statements describing their cutting power printed on their packaging. You'll probably never need a wheel grade above *medium*, but this classification can vary widely from manufacturer to manufacturer. Researching the strength of an abrasive wheel before putting it to use will benefit you and your metal.

Polishing Wheels

You'll use a series of polishing wheels attached to a motorized finishing tool to spread different polishing compounds across a silver piece. Wheels are used for polishing because they're the most effective means of moving compound. A spinning wheel spreads compound with efficiency and with uniformity. Polishing and buffing wheels are designed to grip the compound. It's the compound that removes metal and scratches and cleans the silver, not the polishing wheel. (See page 43 for more information on tripoli, white diamond, and rouge polishing compounds.) Different wheels perform different functions based on their shape and design. Some wheels are stitched, while others are not. Some are better suited for certain jobs or for cleaning in specific locations. For example, it's easier to polish confined areas with a narrow wheel than with one that's wide and flat.

Abrasive wheels for the flexible shaft

Polishing wheels for the flexible shaft

39

THE BASICS

Stitched impregnated polishing wheels

Stitched cotton polishing wheels

Cotton balloon polishing wheels

Stitched muslin polishing wheels

Stitched Impregnated Polishing Wheel

A stitched impregnated wheel is a cutting wheel, usually yellow or purple in color. It's used to remove scratches, light file marks, and other superficial blemishes by cutting away the top metal layer. A stitched impregnated polishing wheel is the best first-stage polishing wheel because it has the most bite. It's stitched in order to keep the wheel stiff to the ends, and it's designed for use with cutting compounds, such as tripoli. The chemical impregnation of the wheel with an abrasive helps grip the compound and keep it on the wheel longer. This is a useful characteristic in the cutting stages, but it can be harmful in the polishing stages. Once scratches are removed, you want to start cleaning the silver with more finesse and less force. You don't want to cut any more metal. At this stage, it's best to switch the style of wheel and type of polishing compound.

Stitched Cotton Wheel

Stitched cotton wheels are indispensable for polishing silver and come in a variety of sizes. With circular stitching coming out from their "button," stitched cotton wheels are stiffer, they hold their shape better, and they're more controllable than a loose, or *balloon*, wheel. But stitched cotton wheels are softer and won't cut as deep as an impregnated wheel. Since stitched cotton wheels aren't chemically impregnated to grip a polishing compound, they release it once it's full of metal residue. If held to the wheel, this residue would scratch the silver. That's why a stitched cotton wheel produces a better finish than an impregnated stitched wheel when used with non-cutting compounds, such as white diamond and rouge. They're very effective for polishing silver if you don't have file or sanding marks to remove.

Cotton Balloon Wheel

Cotton balloon wheels are attached only at the button. Out of all the polishing wheels, they have the least cutting power and force behind them. This loose wheel has much more motion than a stitched wheel. It grips the compound the same way as a stitched cotton wheel, but its layers are more free flowing. The wheel fabric balloons out under pressure. This makes it a great wheel to use on large, open silver pieces with flat surfaces. With practice, these wheels are also fantastic for polishing inside curves, such as those in shallow bowls and dishes. A cotton balloon wheel won't rub or cut the silver as much as a stitched wheel, allowing you to polish pieces without erasing any detail. You must be very careful and always remain alert when using loose wheels; they grab metalwork, especially edges, more easily than any other wheels. This can cause the silver

Muslin balloon polishing wheels

Leather chamois burnishing wheels

to fly and get damaged. Don't even bother trying to increase the pressure of your polishing when using a balloon wheel; you'll only be increasing the likelihood of getting a piece caught.

Stitched Muslin Wheel
Muslin polishing wheels are softer than cotton wheels. They produce the most uniform shine and buff and leave the least pitting and streaking. A stitched muslin wheel is stiffer and offers more control than a balloon muslin wheel.

Muslin Balloon Wheel
A muslin balloon wheel moves like a cotton balloon wheel, and it offers the same amount of control. Its cloth, however, is cleaner and softer, making it better for final finishing. You'll find muslin balloon wheels easiest to use on open and flat

silver surfaces. They work very well with rouge compound. Spinning a clean one with no compound across silver is a wonderful and quick way to wipe off the streaks left by rouge polishing.

Leather Chamois
A leather chamois is a burnishing wheel. It works well on clean hollowware, such as teapots, creamers, and sugar bowls. It's also great for clean flat pieces and pitted large surfaces. When used with rouge compound, a leather chamois brings up silver's highest possible shine. It's crucial that these wheels do not become contaminated, as they cannot be "stepped down" for use with cutting compounds. Using a leather chamois takes practice and care, and you need a clean muslin balloon wheel on a second arbor to whip the finished silver surface

clean. Because these wheels grip hard and fast, they can cause incredible amounts of damage and must be utilized with extreme caution.

Keeping the Polishing Wheels Separate
You must dedicate each polishing wheel you use to a single type of polishing compound. For example, if you intend to use a stitched muslin wheel through each stage of the polishing process—cutting, polishing, and finishing (or tripoli, white diamond, and rouge)—you'll need three separate wheels. A speck of contamination here or there isn't going to render a wheel useless, but, for instance, if you apply tripoli compound to a white diamond wheel, it must become a tripoli wheel. You can step *down* the grit of a wheel from fine to rough (finishing to cutting), but never back *up* again.

Polishing wheel and polishing compound storage system

Storing Polishing Wheels

It's a good practice to keep the polishing wheels physically separate. Labeling your wheels according to compound will help you remember their function. "R" or a red dot can stand for *rouge*; "W" or a white dot for *white diamond*; and "B" or "T" or a brown dot for *tripoli*. Plastic bags provide excellent wheel storage, especially for the rouge wheels. It's imperative to block contamination of any kind to the rouge wheels. Any impurities will show up on your silver, and the wheels will be spoiled. As a wheel ages, you may want to step it down to a more coarse compound and re-code it. If there's an R and a W written on the wheel, it's clear that the wheel has been stepped down. Once you complete one stage of polishing, always remove the wheels from the lathe or flexible shaft and store them before moving onto the next polishing stage.

Preparing New Wheels for the Polishing Lathe

All new polishing wheels must be combed before use. A clean and well-prepared wheel can be the difference between a mediocre polish and a magnificent polish.

WHAT YOU NEED
Hammer
Nails, ¾ inch (1.9 cm)
Wood dowel or stick, ½ inch (1.3 cm) thick
New polishing wheel of your choice
Polishing lathe

WHAT YOU DO

1. Hammer three rows of nails through one end of the wood dowel or stick, spacing each nail ³⁄₁₆ inch (2 mm) apart. Each pointed nail end should stick out of the wood approximately ¼ inch (6 mm), forming a rough comb.

2. Attach a new wheel to the arbor of the polishing lathe. Do not apply any compound to the wheel.

3. Turn on the polishing lathe. Using the comb made in step 1, comb the wheel to remove extra threads, knots, and other particles from the fabric that can scratch, pit, and abrade the metal.

Polishing compounds:
tripoli, white diamond, rouge

4. Turn off the lathe. As shown in the photo, pull out any long threads still hanging on the wheel. (Any threads left hanging will attract extra compound and drag it across the metal, leaving more marks for you to remove.)

Combing a Dirty Polishing Wheel

You'll need to comb a polishing wheel if it gets too sticky or too covered with metal residue. In this circumstance, combing is rubbing a buff comb, the pointed end of a file, or a nail-impregnated dowel or stick against a dirty wheel to break up grimy build-up. After being combed, the wheel regains the flexibility of its cloth.

Using a commercial comb to clean a polishing wheel

Polishing Compounds

The real secret to achieving a dazzling shine is in the silver polishing compounds. These substances do all the work; it's not the force of your arms or the heat of the metal. By correctly using compounds your silver can become absolutely radiant.

Polishing compounds are wax and oil mixed with different abrasive or burnishing compounds that cut, shine, or buff silver. They come in different color-coded grades and are often manufactured in stick form to make identification and application easier. Using a motor-driven wheel to rub a polishing compound across metal is a controlled method of distribution. When polishing silver, you'll employ a sequence of three compounds, from most to least abrasive.

Tripoli Compound

Tripoli compound is the first polishing compound you'll use on a sterling silver piece. Commonly brown in color, tripoli is a cutting compound that actually removes metal. Used properly, tripoli removes small scratches, such as filing marks, without too much difficulty, but it won't repair cuts, dents, or dings. (These problems should be fixed before you start polishing.) Tripoli compound also removes quite a bit of firescale. This compound is best applied first with a stitched impregnated wheel, and then with a plain stitched wheel.

White Diamond Compound

White diamond compound is less abrasive than tripoli, but it's still a cutting compound. You'll use it in the second phase of the polishing process. White diamond makes fine cuts, leaving a brighter surface finish than tripoli. It also removes firescale, but not as fast as tripoli. (I suggest you repolish your work with tripoli compound if you find any firescale spots larger than 1 mm.) In effect, the white diamond compound erases the small cutting marks left by the tripoli. This compound is best applied first with a stitched wheel, and then with a balloon wheel.

Rouge Compound

The final polishing compound, rouge, isn't a cutting compound. It doesn't remove metal. Instead, rouge is a burnishing compound. When repeatedly hit against metal, rouge hardens its surface and brings up its highest shine. To use rouge compound, you need a non-contaminated wheel and a very clean silver piece. If the polishing wheel is not clean, the rouge process will not work. Compared to white diamond, polishing with rouge compound produces a much more noticeable shine. Silver is the most reflective metal on the planet, and, with a proper rouge polishing, you can achieve a shine that grabs the eye unlike anything else. Since polishing with rouge is the last step, you may be tempted to skip it, but, believe me, the results are worth the effort. You will be amazed.

Keeping Polishing Compounds Separate

Since polishing compounds have different abrasive grits, they must be kept apart to preserve their integrity. Mingling compounds leads to contamination. Organize a way to keep the sticks separate because, over time and with repeated rubbing, they'll become difficult to tell apart. Regardless of the compound type, all sticks develop a black covering on their wheel-rubbed areas.

Continually moving a silver piece while polishing

The Polishing Dance

When you polish, always try to keep the silver piece moving. Do your best to make the polishing wheel and the silver piece "dance" with each other. This suggestion applies to every compound. If you concentrate your polishing on only one area, that area will change, and the piece will be transformed. Keeping a piece stationary on the wheel could put waves in the surface of the silver and disturb the look you've worked so hard to achieve.

Basic Lathe Polishing

WHAT YOU NEED

Stitched muslin or cotton wheel, for tripoli polishing compound
Polishing lathe
Tripoli, white diamond, and rouge polishing compounds
Sterling silver piece to be polished
Liquid dishwashing soap
Stitched muslin or cotton wheel, for white diamond polishing compound
Balloon muslin or cotton wheel, for rouge polishing compound
Clean balloon muslin or cotton wheel (optional)

WHAT YOU DO

1. Install the stitched muslin or cotton wheel on the polishing lathe.

2. Turn on the lathe and spin the wheel against the tripoli compound (see top photo, below). Rub the sterling silver piece against the wheel to remove surface imperfections and scratches on the metal (see bottom photo, below).

3. Thoroughly rinse the silver in hot water with liquid dishwashing soap to remove excess polishing compound (see top photo, below). Look at the silver piece in good light (see bottom photo, below). If it's clear of blemishes, clean your polishing station, store the tripoli supplies, and proceed to step 4. If the silver surface is still marred, repeat steps 2 and 3.

AT SOME POINT, YOUR POLISHING MACHINE MAY SEEM TO HAVE A MIND OF ITS OWN AND NOT SEEM TO BE IN A GOOD MOOD. IT JUST KEEPS GRABING YOUR WORK. YOU KEEP GOING AND IT KEEPS THROWING. GETTING FRUSTRATED AND AGGRAVATED WON'T CHANGE WHATEVER'S HAPPENING. NEITHER WILL PRESSING ON WITH YOUR WORK. UNDER THESE CIRCUMSTANCES, OFTEN THE BEST THING TO DO IS TO STOP COMPLETELY, TAKE A BREAK, WALK AWAY FROM THE PROJECT, AND COME BACK LATER.

4. Place a stitched muslin or cotton wheel on the arbor of the polishing lathe. Turn on the lathe and spin the wheel against the white diamond compound. Rub the sterling silver piece against the wheel as shown in the photo. Rinse the silver in hot soapy water.

5. Check the silver piece for marks and blemishes (see photo). If there are scratches that the white diamond won't remove, repeat steps 1 through 4. Keep repeating these steps until the compounds have done their best job. Clean your polishing station and store the white diamond supplies.

6. Attach a balloon muslin or cotton wheel to the polishing lathe arbor. (If you have a double-arbor wheel, attach a clean and compound-free balloon wheel to the second side.) Rub the rouge compound on the balloon wheel (see top photo, below). Burnish the silver (see center photo, below). Occasionally dust the piece with the clean balloon wheel (if you're using one) to remove excess compound and prevent streaking as shown in the bottom photo, below. Wash the silver piece in hot soapy water, and then examine it in good light. Repeat the burnishing process with the rouge compound and dusting the silver until you

achieve the shine you desire. Clean your polishing station, and store the rouge supplies.

Replenishing Polishing Compounds

As you polish, the compounds will need replenishing. There are several ways to tell if a wheel needs more compound:
• When the surface of the polishing wheel looks metallic
• When the wheel fabric is sticking together
• When the wheel doesn't appear to be doing its job

Physical Fitness & Polishing Safety

Each person approaches polishing differently, but successful polishing does require the proper use of the entire upper body. You need to always be physically healthy and mentally alert. If you polish for too long, you'll lose concentration, an object could fly, and your back and arms will ache for days afterward.

GOOD TIMES TO TAKE A BREAK FROM POLISHING

• When you get tired
• When you have trouble concentrating
• When your vision is failing
• When you're uncomfortable and need to shift positions
• When you become frustrated
• When you become aggravated with the machine

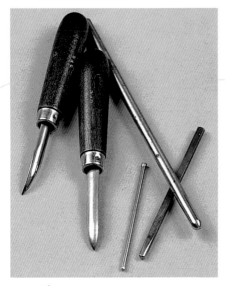

From left: commercial burnishers, handmade burnishers

Burnisher

To burnish is to manually rub metal with a hard surface. Because it moves metal in a quiet and clean way that no other tool can replicate, a burnisher is a wonderful finishing tool every silversmith should have. It can perform a multitude of tasks, such as securing a bezel setting and removing or hiding pits and marks. The most important qualities of a good burnisher are smoothness and cleanliness. You can purchase burnishers of various sizes and shapes from any jewelry supplier, or you can make one of your own. Some people polish old railroad stakes or large nails to use as burnishers. Others cut or grind a scrap brass rod into the shape they desire, and then polish it to a high shine. You also can hammer one end of a thick nail into a handle, and then clean and polish its opposite end to make a simple burnisher.

Tarnish

I'm often asked about tarnish—how to get rid of it, and how to keep it away. Maintaining the appearance of sterling silver is easier than most people think. Here's a description of what tarnish is and how best to combat it.

Tarnish is the reaction of metal's copper content to oxygen and sulfur in the air. The major culprit is sulfur. If you live in a sulfur-rich environment, you'll struggle with tarnish more than people who live with lower sulfur levels. (A rural environment with few cars has less sulfur trapped in its air than a congested metropolis.)

First and foremost, use your silver. Sterling silver that gets regular use and regular cleaning tarnishes less. A regular cleaning can be as simple as washing your pieces in soapy water with a soft sponge. Don't use a scrubbing sponge, and don't use abrasive soaps. It's much harder to keep a nice finish on silver that isn't used and washed often.

You can also deter tarnish by using impregnated cloths and papers. These sulfur-absorbing materials are fantastic, but their effectiveness won't last forever. You can seal small silver pieces in a plastic bag with a piece of anti-tarnish paper or wrap your silver in anti-tarnish cloths before storing it. You can even put sulfur-absorbing cloth or paper in a cupboard behind silver that's on display. This way, the silver is out where people can see it, but it's in an anti-tarnish, low-sulfur environment. All absorbent anti-tarnish cloths and papers will eventually become saturated and no longer protect your silver. Just remember to replace them as needed.

If your silver's shine has faded, use a leather chamois and silver polish to get it back. I prefer slightly thick liquid polish to paste. Put a drop or two of the polish directly on the silver, rub it around the surface with a piece of leather chamois, and then wipe off the polish with a clean chamois. A leather chamois is often used to buff or wax cars. This type of cloth isn't abrasive, and it's absolutely fantastic for bringing back silver's shine. The thick liquid silver polish rubs on and wipes off with ease, and you'll be amazed at the amount of tarnish it can remove (and at how much tarnish was there to begin with!).

Burnishing the edge of a silver form

Project Kits

The silversmithing projects in this book all come with lists that indicate the materials, hammers, and tools you need to complete them. There are other items required on a regular basis that I've organized into two "kits." To shorten the length of the lists with each project, when these kits are needed, you'll be referred back to this page.

SOLDERING KIT

Heat-resistant soldering station
Oxy-propane torch
Striker
Flux, paste or liquid
Flux brush or spray bottle
Pickle (sulfuric acid) bath, alum, or citric acid
Slow cooker
Copper tongs
Soldering surfaces, such as a turntable, tripod, or ceramic plate
Solder (refer to project directions for types)
Wire clippers
Tweezers
Fire extinguisher
Safety goggles

POLISHING KIT

Flexible shaft
Polishing lathe (optional, but recommended for large projects)
Abrasive wheels to fit flexible shaft and/or polishing lathe
Stitched muslin or cotton polishing wheels to fit flexible shaft and/or polishing lathe
Balloon muslin or cotton polishing wheels to fit flexible shaft and/or polishing lathe
Tripoli polishing compound
White diamond polishing compound
Rouge polishing compound
Liquid dishwashing soap
Soft cotton cloths
Respirator or dust mask
Safety goggles

THE BASICS

The Projects

With a basic understanding of silversmithing materials, tools, and techniques, you can create many objects that are both beautiful and functional. Begin with simple hammering, filing, and folding to handcraft the handsome Money Clip. Intermediate projects, such as the Condiment Dish and the Forged Fork & Spoon, give you the opportunity to strengthen your skills and learn new ones, such as sinking and forging. Later in this chapter, you'll encounter more advanced projects, such as the Cocktail Shaker and the Creamer & Sugar Bowl. When crafting these you'll fully experience the joy and satisfaction of moving a lot of metal!

Money Clip

You get a lot of bang for your buck from this simple and stylish accessory.

WHAT YOU NEED
Materials
Sterling silver sheet, 18 gauge,
   1 x 4 inches (2.5 x 10.2 cm)

Hammers
Planishing hammer (optional)
Rawhide mallet

Other Tools
Needle files or sandpaper block
Swage block
Steel dowel
Flat-head pliers
Files

Kits
Polishing kit, page 47

Techniques
Filing, page 15
Planishing, page 28
Polishing, page 44

WHAT YOU DO
Preparing the Silver Sheet

1 Use a needle file or a sandpaper block to smooth all the edges of the 18-gauge sterling silver sheet. Round the corners of the sheet.

2 Decide if you want the money clip to have a planished or a mirror surface. (I recommend beginning silversmiths create a planished surface. This process requires less cleaning and teaches you more techniques. If you choose to create a mirror surface, move to step 3.) To planish the surface, place the sterling silver piece on top of the swage block. Use the slightly domed face of the planishing hammer to hit the silver where it is in contact with the swage block. Hammer rows of little marks on the metal. As you planish, the silver will move and curve upwards. Keep hammering in straight rows.

Creating the Money Clip Form

3 Measure and mark a centerline across the width of the metal. Measure 2 to 3 mm to one side of the centerline, and mark a second line. This is where you'll bend the metal. (If you bend the metal in the center, the money clip won't have the lip and ledge it needs to properly function.) Hold the piece of marked metal against the swage block or the edge of your worktable with the marked side down. Align the second line with the edge of the swage block or table. Begin bending the metal around the edge to form a 90-degree angle.

4 Position the steel dowel inside the curve of the bent metal. Place the long side of the metal down on the table. (The short metal side will bend up in the air.) Holding down the long metal side, bend the short side over the dowel and down to make the basic money clip form (see photo 1).

STERLING WORDS

IF YOU PLANISH IN SMALL AND MEASURED INCREMENTS, YOU CAN CATCH UNEVEN HAMMER STROKES MORE EASILY.

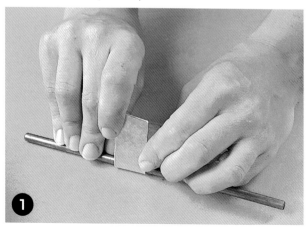

1

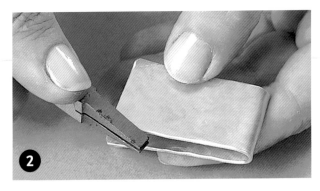

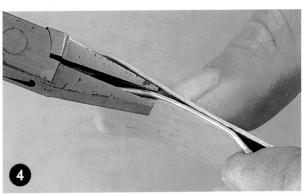

5 As shown in photo 2, use the flat-nose pliers to bend up a 1- to 2-mm section on both edges of the shorter side of the clip.

6 Set the clip and the dowel on the table, long side down. While holding the dowel inside the clip, hit the metal with the rawhide mallet (see photo 3). Use the mallet to push the two ends of the metal around the dowel and closer to each other. (The two edges won't meet because of the nature of the metal. It's slightly springy, and, as it hardens, it tries to bounce back. Hammering the ends won't get the two sides to meet, but they will if you work closer to the middle.) The dowel helps to form a nice uniform curve. Hammering the metal on the swage block and curving it around the steel dowel hardens the metal so it will spring when used to hold money.

7 Using the flat-nose pliers, grip one side of the curve in the money clip. The nose of the pliers should only be about 1 cm in from the edge of the metal. As shown in photo 4, twist the pliers to expand the arch of the curve and to bend the ends toward each other. Work the arch of the money clip, not its edges. Repeat this step on the other side of the clip.

Finishing & Polishing the Money Clip

8 If the money clip edges aren't straight, file the lower edges flush.

9 Attach a small stitched muslin wheel to the motorized polishing tool of your choice. Clean and polish the surface and edges of the money clip with tripoli compound to remove any scratches and abrasions. Rinse and dry the clip. Clean your polishing area and store the tripoli supplies.

10 Attach a stitched muslin wheel to the motorized polishing tool of your choice. Carefully polish the money clip with the white diamond compound. Rinse it in hot soapy water. Clean your polishing area and store the white diamond supplies.

11 Attach a stitched muslin wheel to the motorized polishing tool of your choice. Carefully polish the money clip with the rouge compound. Rinse the clip in hot soapy water. Clean your polishing area and store the rouge compound. Repeat this polishing sequence as often as needed to achieve the desired polish.

Hammered Belt Buckle

A little hammering, soldering, and polishing are all it takes for you to create a one-of-kind belt buckle.

WHAT YOU NEED

Materials
Sterling silver sheet, 18 gauge,
   2 x 3 inches (5 x 7.6 cm)
Sterling silver wire, 16 gauge,
   2½ inches (6.4 cm)
Hard solder

Hammers
Sinking hammer
Planishing hammer

Other Tools
Files
Sandpaper (optional)
Scribe (optional)
Sandbag or wooden dapping block
Flat mushroom stake
Jeweler's saw and saw blades
Calipers

Kits
Soldering kit, page 47
Polishing kit, page 47

Techniques
Filing, page 15
Sinking, page 29
Planishing, page 28
Sawing, page 12
Soldering, page 35
Polishing, page 44
Piercing (optional), page 13

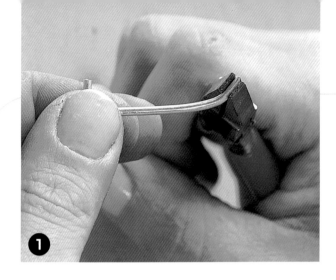

WHAT YOU DO

Doming the Buckle

1 Use a file or sandpaper to smooth the edges of the 2 x 3-inch (5 x 7.6 cm) sterling silver rectangle.

2 On the back side of the rectangle, mark straight lines 1 cm inside each edge. These are guidelines for the sinking hammer. (You can mark these lines with a scribe if you want. Since they're on the back of the buckle, they won't be seen.)

3 Place the sterling silver rectangle on a sandbag or on a wooden dapping block with its guidelines facing up. Use the sinking hammer to hit the silver on the marked lines. The edges of the buckle will start to bend in, forming a shallow dish.

4 Turn over the buckle and place it on the flat mushroom stake. Use the curved edge of the stake for the curved areas of the buckle. Planish and shape the entire buckle surface, lifting it so its edges sit flat on the surface of the stake while hammering. This hardens and stabilizes the silver into a strong buckle. Its shallow dish shape makes a stronger form than if it were simply a flat buckle. You should now have a buckle that's fully formed and ready for soldering and finishing.

Creating the Post & Belt Keeper

5 Use the jeweler's saw to cut a ½-inch (1.3 cm) length of the 16-gauge sterling silver wire to use as the buckle's post. Use the remaining wire for the buckle's belt keeper.

6 Measure 5 mm in from one end of the longer wire, and bend it at a 90-degree angle. Measure 1¼ inches (3.2 cm) down the wire from the first bend, and bend a second 90-degree angle, forming a U shape (see photo 1). Cut off the end of the second bend so both wire ends measure 5 mm.

Soldering the Wires to the Buckle

7 Place the buckle face down on your soldering station. If you can no longer see the guidelines drawn in step 2, use the calipers to remeasure and re-mark them so you'll know where to attach the post and belt keeper. Place the post 1 cm in from one end of the buckle. Center the keeper on the buckle's width, 1 cm in from its horizontal edges.

8 When soldering the wire elements to the back side of the buckle, they should be straight, centered, and at the appropriate angles. Hold the pieces in place with pins or tweezers as needed, and flux the buckle and wires. Concentrate on heating the larger surface, the buckle, instead of heating the smaller surfaces, the wires. As shown in photo 2, hard-solder the wires to the belt buckle. Pickle, rinse, and dry it.

Polishing the Belt Buckle

9 Use a coarse wheel, a sanding wheel, or a green kitchen scrub with abrasive cleanser to begin removing the firescale from the back side of the buckle. You could also use an abrasive kitchen cleanser on a toothbrush with liquid dishwashing soap. This rough polishing quickly creates a uniform silver surface and appearance, giving the back side of the buckle a beautiful white finish without the time or effort of a full polish.

10 Polishing the front of the buckle is an easy job, but you must pay close attention to its edges. Attach a small stitched muslin wheel to the motorized polishing tool of your choice. Clean and polish the surface and edges of the belt buckle with tripoli compound to remove any scratches and abrasions. Rinse and dry the buckle. Clean your polishing area and store the tripoli supplies.

11 Attach a stitched muslin wheel to the motorized polishing tool of your choice. Carefully polish the buckle with the white diamond compound. Rinse it in hot soapy water. Clean your polishing area and store the white diamond supplies.

12 Attach a stitched muslin wheel to the motorized polishing tool of your choice. Carefully polish the buckle with the rouge compound. Rinse the holder in hot soapy water. Clean your polishing area and store the rouge compound. Repeat this polishing sequence as often as needed to achieve the desired polish.

Variations

You can jazz up a silver belt buckle by piercing and cutting out a decorative pattern, but you'll need to carefully plan the design. If you take away too much metal, the buckle won't be strong enough. Also give plenty of consideration to where you locate the post and belt keeper. These elements must be attached to a very solid surface.

You can pierce the silver before or after you shape the buckle. I prefer piercing first. If you follow this order, keep in mind that the hammering will change the design. If you've created a very specific design, I recommend piercing after you shape the silver, but before you solder it. Also, closely watch the piercings as you solder. The thinned areas of the buckle are more likely to melt or warp.

Candleholder

To dress up your candles with a shining silver spiral, coil a strip around a dowel and solder it to a shallow dish.

WHAT YOU NEED

Materials

Sterling silver disk, 18 gauge, 3 inches (7.6 cm) in diameter*

Sterling silver sheet, 18 or 20 gauge, 2/5 x 5½ inches (1 x 14 cm)

Hard solder

Hammers

Sinking hammer

Planishing hammer

Other Tools

Compass

Sandbag or dapping block

T-stake or flat mushroom stake (optional)

Files

Needle files

Wood or metal dowel, approximately 20 mm in diameter

Vise

Jeweler's saw and saw blades

Kits

Polishing kit, page 47

Soldering kit, page 47

*You can order a precut disk from a metal supplier, or you can order a 3-inch (7.6 cm) sterling silver square and cut the disk yourself. Since you may have to pay a fabrication charge for a precut disk, it may be more economical in the long run to purchase the square (and you can use the leftover scraps later!).

Techniques

Sawing (optional), page 12

Sinking, page 29

Planishing, page 28

Filing, page 15

Soldering, page 35

Polishing, page 44

Before You Begin

When designing a candleholder, you need to determine what kind and size of candle you want to feature. This design is for a standard tapered candle. If you want to alter this project to accommodate another candle size or style, simply revise the silver and dowel measurements.

WHAT YOU DO

Sinking the Bowl

1 Open the compass to 1 cm. Run it along the outside edge of the 3-inch (7.6 cm) sterling silver disk. This marked line is the guide for your hammering.

2 Set the silver disk on the sandbag or the dapping block. Using the sinking hammer, hit the disk along the marked line. Its edges will raise as you hammer, forming a small silver dish. One sinking turn around the disk should achieve the desired depth of the dish.

3 Rest the silver dish on a T-stake, on the curved edge of a flat mushroom stake, or on the edge of a planishing hammer. Use a planishing hammer to planish out the sinking marks and work the curve.

Constructing the Spiral

4 File the edges of the thin 2/5 x 5½-inch (1 x 14 cm) sterling silver strip. Attach a small stitched muslin wheel to the lathe or the flexible shaft and give the strips a light polish with the tripoli compound. This makes the final cleaning easier. Rinse and dry the strip.

5 Place the wood or metal dowel in the vise. Wrap the ²/₅ x 5½-inch (1 x 14 cm) silver strip around and up the dowel to form a spiral (see photo 1). Carefully remove the silver spiral from the dowel.

6 Select one end of the silver spiral to attach to the silver dish. Mark a straight line across this end that will sit flush on the dish. Use the jeweler's saw to cut off the silver below the marked line. Slowly cut and sand this end until it fits the dish. (If you're having trouble, you can tap the end of the spiral back flat, cut off the end with the jeweler's saw, and then reshape the spiral around the dowel as described in step 5.)

STERLING WORDS

IF YOU DON'T LIKE A PIECE,
GUESS WHAT?
YOU CAN CHANGE IT!
ISN'T SILVERSMITHING GREAT?

Soldering the Bowl & Spiral

7 Line up the spiral candle holder and the silver dish so they're flush. Flux the seam area, light the torch, and heat the entire surface. You may put the pallions of hard solder on the candle holder after you flux and before you heat, or you can apply them as you solder. When the solder balls up, it's about to flow and connect the candleholder elements. If you solder the seams unevenly, use the heat of the torch to "pull" the solder where it needs to flow. Pickle the fully soldered candleholder. Rinse and dry it.

8 Use needle files, small pieces of sandpaper, or a flexible shaft with an abrasive attachment to clean off excess solder from the seam as needed. (Well-soldered seams are nearly invisible and don't require much cleaning.)

Polishing the Candleholder

9 Attach a stitched muslin wheel to the lathe and polish the candleholder with the tripoli compound to remove firescale. Polish carefully, especially in hard-to-reach areas. Remember to polish the candleholder's edges, making sure the wheels are always going with the metal. Figure out how to best hold the candleholder in order to clean its corners. Most importantly, take your time and remain alert. Rinse the candleholder with hot water. Clean your polishing area and store the tripoli supplies.

Tip: Tight areas, such as the space within the spiral, can be difficult to polish. Always approach these challenges with patience and care. To determine what areas the polishing wheel will reach, try placing it into the space with its power off. Once you know where you can polish and with which tools, you can more easily overcome polishing obstacles.

10 Attach a stitched muslin wheel to the lathe and carefully polish the candleholder with white diamond compound. Rinse it in hot soapy water. Clean your polishing area, and store the white diamond supplies.

11 Attach a stitched muslin wheel (and one clean balloon wheel if possible) to the lathe, and polish the candleholder with rouge compound. If you're working on a double-arbor lathe, as you polish the vase, quickly brush it against the clean balloon wheel to remove any streaking compound. When the candleholder is completely polished, a final buffing against a clean balloon wheel will give it a bright final sheen. Rinse in hot soapy water, and pat the candleholder dry.

Business Card Holder

Make a favorable first impression by using this sterling silver business card holder with an elegant pierced motif.

WHAT YOU NEED

Materials
Sterling silver sheet, 18 gauge,
   2½ x 3¾ inches (6.4 x 9.5 cm)
Photocopied design template of your
   choice, page 156

Hammers
Rawhide or wooden mallet
Planishing hammer

Other Tools
Jeweler's saw and saw blades
Swage block or anvil

Center punch
Chasing hammer
Drill bit, 1 mm
Needle files
Steel dowel, ½ inch (1.3 cm)
   in diameter
Flat-nose pliers
Abrasive kitchen or tile cleanser
Toothbrush

Kits
Polishing kit, see page 47

Techniques
Transferring designs, page 10
Piercing, page 13
Sawing, page 12
Filing, page 15
Polishing, page 44

WHAT YOU DO
Plotting & Cutting Out the Design

1 Transfer the photocopied design template onto the 2½ x 3¾-inch (6.4 x 9.5 cm) sterling silver sheet.

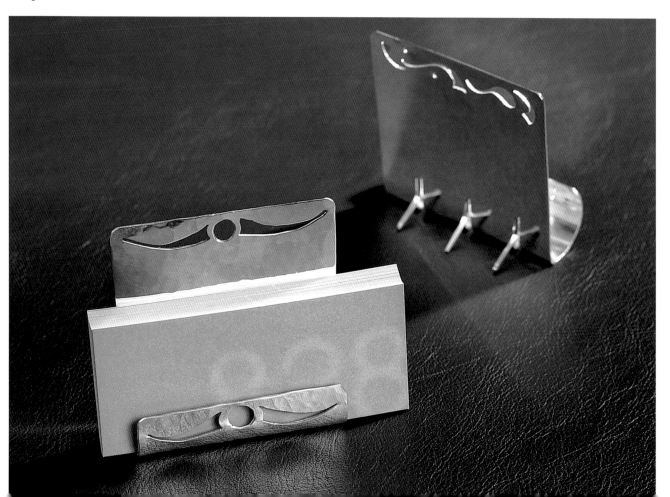

2 Measure and mark two parallel bending positions on the metal as shown in figure 1. Make the first line across the sheet's width 2½ inches (6.4 cm) in from one end (line A). Make the second line (line B) 3 inches (7.6 cm) in from the same end. This leaves two outer sections of metal, one 2½ inches (6.4 cm) and the second ¾ inch (1.9 cm).

3 Follow figure 2 to plot the following sequence of marks:
- Make three pairs of marks on line A: one pair in the center of the line and a pair ½ inch (1.3 cm) inside each metal edge. Space the lines in each pair approximately 1 mm apart.
- Make identical marks on line B.
- Draw straight and parallel lines across the metal to connect the marks on line A with those on line B.
- Extend the lines an additional ½ inch (1.3 cm) past line A.
- Draw a line connecting each pair centered between and parallel to line A and line B.

4 Use the jeweler's saw to cut out the decorative edges of the business card holder, following the lines of the transferred design.

5 One at a time, pierce and saw out the business card holder's interior decorative shapes. Place the silver on the swage block or anvil. Use the center punch and chasing hammer to dimple the point on the design you want to drill. Using a 1-mm bit, drill a hole at the dimple. Thread the saw blade through this hole and cut out the design. Repeat this procedure to cut out all the designs. File the cut edges smooth with the needle files.

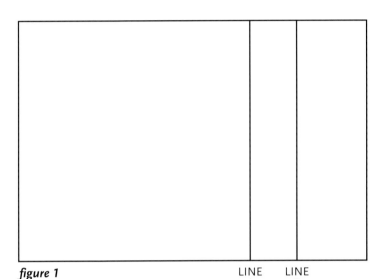

figure 1 LINE A LINE B

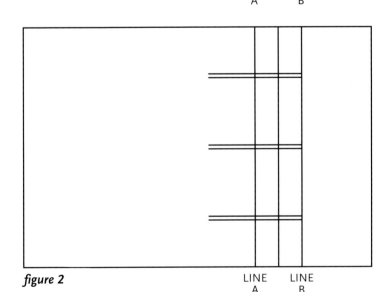

figure 2 LINE A LINE B

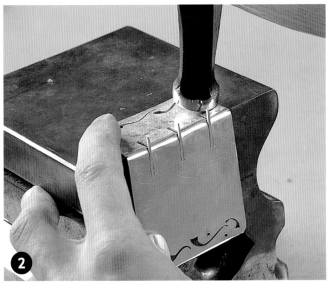

Forming the Legs

6 For the holder to sit upright at an angle that will support business cards, it needs back legs. The easiest way to create legs is to cut them free from the existing metal. You'll be pulling the supporting legs from the bottom of the holder so they won't affect its appearance. Place the holder on the swage block or anvil and use the center punch to dimple the three last points (just above line B) marked in step 3. Use a 1-mm bit to drill the dimples. (This bit should just fit within each set of marked lines.) As shown in photo 1, use the saw to cut two straight lines away from each drilled hole, following the extended lines drawn in step 3.

7 To ensure a flat-sitting holder, measure to make sure all of the legs start the same distance away from the bending lines. If they don't, use the jeweler's saw to even the legs. Measure from the pierced lines to the drill points. This should be about a ¾-inch (1.9 cm) space. Use the needle files to clean up the pierced ends to match each other, and to even their length. These are the card holder's three legs.

Shaping the Holder

8 Place the card holder on the swage block or anvil. Align line A with the edge of the block and use your hands to begin bending the metal over its edge. (The cutout legs don't need to bend with the metal at this time. Let them stick out for a while.) Using the rawhide or wooden mallet, lightly hammer the bend of the metal while it's on the block. To form a more precise 90-degree angle, change to the planishing hammer and gently tap either side of the bend (see photo 2).

9 Move the card holder forward on the swage block or anvil so the angle made in step 8 slightly sticks out past the edge of the block. Using the rawhide or wood-

3

en mallet, tap all the way across the holder's surface until the metal finally "gives," conforming to a 90-degree edge.

10 Place the back side of the card holder on your worktable. (The legs aren't yet in their supporting positions.) Rest the ½-inch (1.3 cm) dowel against the end of the bent metal. Bend the metal around the dowel with your hands to make the final lift on the remaining bending line (line B). When you've bent it as much as you can by hand, change to the mallet. Tap where you want the metal to move and where the metal is not resting on or touching the dowel (see photo 3). If the curve isn't forming the way you want, you can use the planishing hammer. Since you're working on a curve, use the flatter side of the hammer. Its marks won't be as pronounced as the more curved hammer surface. Push the metal until the front and the back sides of the holder have parallel edges, and the shape will hold cards.

11 Use the flat-nose pliers to grab one of the card holder legs. Pull it away from the back side of the holder until it sits at a pleasing angle. Repeat this process for the remaining legs. Adjust the legs as needed until they sit at the same angle, allowing the card holder to lean back and be stable (slightly less than perpendicular to the back side).

Polishing the Holder

12 Attach a small stitched muslin wheel to the motorized polishing tool of your choice. Clean and polish the surface and outside contour of the card holder with tripoli compound to remove any scratches and abrasions. If the card holder has deeper scratches than tripoli can remove, switch to sandpaper or a mildly abrasive wheel attachment.

13 Use an abrasive kitchen or tile cleanser and a toothbrush to polish inside the card holder's pierced designs. Brush inside the cutouts using small circular motions. The silver will take on an attractive pearly white satin finish.

14 Complete the card holder's tripoli polish. Rinse it clean and let dry. Clean your polishing area and store the tripoli supplies.

15 Attach a stitched muslin wheel to the motorized polishing tool of your choice. Carefully polish the card holder with the white diamond compound. Rinse the holder in hot soapy water. Clean your polishing area and store the white diamond supplies.

16 Attach a stitched muslin wheel to the motorized polishing tool of your choice. Carefully polish the card holder with the rouge compound. Rinse the holder in hot soapy water. Clean your polishing area and store the rouge compound. Repeat this polishing sequence as often as needed to achieve the desired polish.

Variations
After creating this project, why not make other business card holders with customized designs? You could alter the shape of the back and front edges, alter the pierced motif, or change the surface texture. Adding a monogram to personalize the holder would be an especially thoughtful touch. There are countless opportunities to expand on this design.

Cuff Bracelet

As this highly textured bracelet shows, creating dramatic art to wear can be part of a silversmith's repertoire.

WHAT YOU NEED

Materials
Sterling silver sheet, 18 gauge,
  1 x 5⅛ inches (2.5 x 13 cm)

Hammers
Forging hammer
Planishing hammer
Rawhide or wooden mallet (optional)

Other Tools
Files
Needle files
Scribe or compass
Swage block or anvil

Brass or steel brush
T-stake, workbench, or broom handle

Kits
Polishing kit, page 47

Techniques
Filing, page 15
Forging, page 23
Planishing, page 28
Polishing, page 44

WHAT YOU DO
Filing & Forging the Silver

1 Use the files to smooth the edges of the 1 x 5⅛-inch (2.5 x 13 cm) sterling silver sheet. Use a scribe or a compass to mark a centerline down the length of the silver. (You'll use this guideline to direct your hammering.)

STERLING WORDS

THIS CUFF BRACELET HAS A FREE FORM WITH LOOSE ROLLING EDGES. IT'S A GREAT PIECE FOR HAMMERING PRACTICE.

Rolling & Tapping Down the Silver Edges

2 Place the marked silver sheet on the swage block or anvil. Use the forging hammer to hit down the length of the silver on one side of the marked line. Hammer down the opposite side of the line. (Don't worry if you accidently hammer over the centerline. It's a guide, not a strict dividing point.) Only hammer one side of the silver sheet. The side facing the swage block or anvil becomes the inside of the bracelet and doesn't need to be hammered.

3 Place the hammered side of the silver sheet against the vertical edge of the swage block or anvil. Adjust the silver so one edge is approximately ⅛ inch (3 mm) above the hammering surface. Use a forging hammer, a planishing hammer, or a rawhide or wooden mallet to hit the edge of the silver, pushing it over the edge of the hammering surface (see photo 1). Repeat this process to "roll" both edges of the silver. It will have a flattened **U** or a **[** shape.

4 Rest the silver on the hammering surface with the textured side facing up. Use the hammer with which you're most comfortable and you have the most control to tap down the bent edges toward the textured surface of the silver as shown in photo 2. Stop hammering once the bent edges are nearly flat. If you're not already using it, switch to the planishing hammer and complete hammering the edges. (The difference in texture between the folded edge and the forged surface is a beautiful contrast.) File the ends of the silver smooth.

STERLING WORDS

FOR SUCH A LARGE PIECE OF JEWELRY, THE CUFF BRACELET IS SURPRISINGLY COMFORTABLE AND LIGHTWEIGHT.

Bending the Cuff

5 Place the silver over the edge of a T-stake, a workbench, or a broom handle and use your hands to bend the cuff into a long C shape (see photo 3). Try on the cuff to see if you like its form. Make sure the wrist opening is large enough and adjust as needed. (Because it's a cuff, the metal can be bent more or less as needed at any time.)

Polishing the Silver

6 This project requires only light cleaning. You'll polish only the folded edges, the back side, and the outer ends of the silver. Once polishing is complete, the silver should have no burrs or file marks. Attach a stitched muslin wheel to the flexible shaft. Apply tripoli compound to the wheel and clean the edges of the silver, taking care not to polish or remove its hammered texture. Polish the unfolded ends extra smooth, as they'll have repeated contact with the wearer. (You can slightly taper the cuff ends prior to polishing them if you wish.) Lightly polish the back side of the silver to a shiny finish.

7 Working under running water with liquid dishwashing soap, use the brass or steel brush to shine the textured areas of the silver. This process appears to lightly polish the textured areas, but is actually lightly burnishing them. (On a smooth or mirrored surface, the brass or steel brush would reduce the silver's shine and reflection, but on a textured surface, it accomplishes the reverse.) Rinse and dry the silver. Clean your polishing area and store the tripoli supplies.

8 Use the flexible shaft with a stitched wheel and white diamond compound to repolish the silver's folded edges, making the contrast brighter and the piece's overall look more finished. Rinse and dry the silver. Clean your polishing area and store the white diamond supplies.

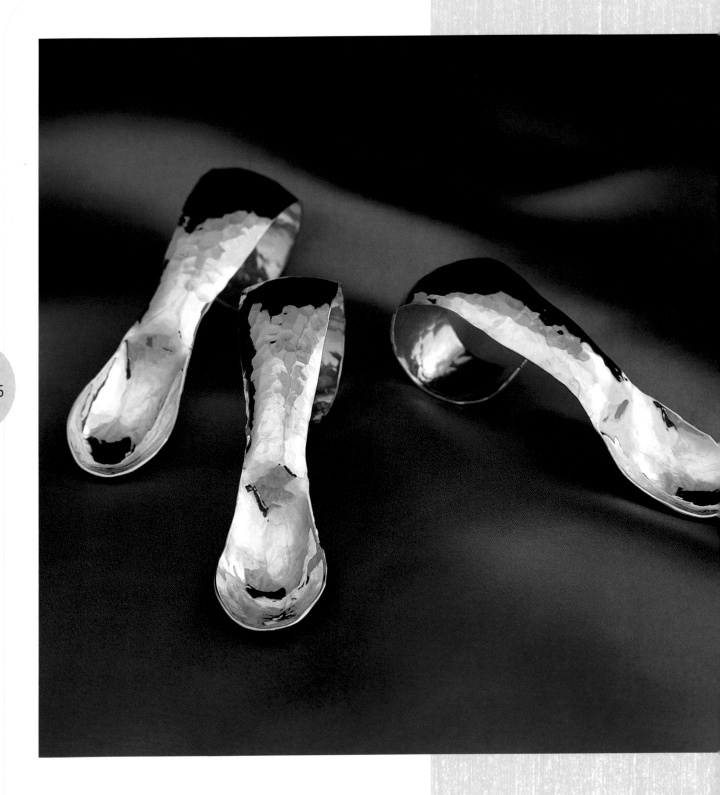

Baby Spoon

*Try out your new hammering skills to sink
a spoon bowl and planish its handle.*

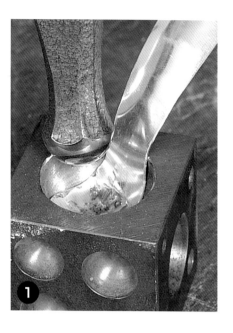

WHAT YOU NEED

Materials

Sterling silver sheet, 18 gauge,
 1 x 6 inches (2.5 x 15.2 cm)
Photocopied template, page 156

Hammers

Sinking hammer
Planishing hammer

Other Tools

Jeweler's saw and saw blades
Files
Needle files
Sandbag
Dapping block or carved wood block
 with 1-inch (2.5 cm) cavity
Dapping tool (optional)
T-stake (optional)
Vise (optional)
Sandpaper block (optional)

Kits

Soldering kit, page 47
Polishing kit, page 47

Techniques

Transferring designs, page 10
Sawing, page 12
Filing, page 15
Sinking, page 29
Planishing, page 28
Polishing, page 44

WHAT YOU DO

1 Transfer the photocopied template
onto the 1 x 6-inch (2.5 x 15.2 cm) sterling silver sheet. Use the jeweler's saw
to cut out the transferred shape. File the
cut edges and anneal the metal.

Doming the Handle

2 Place the annealed metal on the sandbag. Using the sinking hammer, hit the
metal in the center of the spoon handle.
Continue hammering on alternate sides
of the centerpoint, working your way
toward the ends, as shown in figure 1.
This action should achieve a light doming, bringing the outer edges of the handle up and the inner surface down.

Sinking the Spoon Face

3 Hold the spoon face over a 1-inch
(2.5 cm) cavity in the dapping block or
carved wood block. Hold the handle of
the spoon with its dome facing up. Using
a dapping tool or a sinking hammer,
dap or sink the face of the spoon to form
a depression as shown in photo 1. Make
the cavity large enough to accommodate
the pad of your thumb. This is the right
shape and form for a baby spoon. (If your
hands are very large, use your index
finger. If they're very small, approximate
the size.)

7 5 3 1 2 4 6 8

figure 1

THE PROJECTS

Bending the Handle
& Planishing the Spoon

4 Use a T-stake or a dap to bend the handle. If you use a dap, secure it in a vise with its curved end up. Gently rest the area of the handle that's nearest the spoon face on the curve of the dap and begin to shape the handle with the planishing hammer (see photo 2). Start on the handle's centerline, and then work on its edges. Gently move the spoon as you hammer, accentuating the curve of the handle. As you hammer down the length of the spoon's handle, you'll have to rock and move it more because there is a wider silver surface to transform. This is as much a planishing job as a forming job. The curve is already formed in the metal; you're simply refining it.

5 The handle bends around under itself near its widest part. Creating this bend is the trickiest part of this project because the bend wants to diminish the dome made in step 2. In order to keep the dome uniform, use harder hammer strokes on the sides than you used on the rest of the spoon. Holding the spoon firm and keeping the surface of the stake in the center of the handle, hit down hardest on the side edges as shown in photo 3. This allows you to move the metal on the sides and maintain the proper dome. If you planish the entire spoon and the bend isn't where you want it, you can continue to work on this area. If the bend fights back too hard or won't move, re-anneal the spoon and continue working until you're satisfied.

6 To further shape the spoon face, flip it over and planish its back side over a dap or a T-stake. If the spoon face is already properly roughed out, use this step to resurface and clean it.

Finishing & Polishing the Spoon

7 Use files, needle files, or even a block of sandpaper to smooth the edges of the bowl of the spoon. Work slowly and steadily to create a flat and uniform edge and to remove all burrs. If you use a sandpaper block, you can rest the spoon face upside down on the edge of the block and rub it back and forth.

8 Use the flexible shaft with a stitched muslin or a felt wheel and tripoli compound to polish the face of the spoon. (If you have a polishing lathe, you can use it only on the larger surfaces of the spoon.) As you polish, periodically wipe off excess compound to check your progress. Polish the remaining surface of the spoon, including behind the curve of the handle. Rinse the spoon in hot soapy water, and let dry. Clean your polishing area and store the tripoli supplies.

9 Use the flexible shaft with a stitched wheel and white diamond compound to polish the spoon. Rinse and dry the silver. Clean your polishing area and store the white diamond supplies.

Bud Vase

A silver bud vase can be as beautiful as the flowers it holds. To create this one, you'll join a forged tube with a shallow sunken dish.

WHAT YOU NEED

Materials
Sterling silver sheet, 18 gauge,
   3 x 3 inches (7.6 x 7.6 cm)
Sterling silver sheet, 18 gauge,
   4½ x 2 inches (11.4 x 5 cm)
Hard solder
Pallion solder, medium or easy

Hammers
Sinking hammer
Planishing hammer
Narrow forging hammer
Rawhide or wooden mallet (optional)

Other Tools
Compass
Jeweler's saw and saw blades
Sandbag
Files
Needle files
Wood dowel or gently sloping mushroom
   stake, 2 inches (5 cm) in diameter
Vise
Scribe
Hammering block with a V- or
   U-shape channel
Binding wire (optional)
Steel dowel, ½ inch (1.3 cm) in diameter
Sawdust or paper towel

Kits

Polishing kit, page 47
Soldering kit, page 47

Techniques

Sawing, page 12
Sinking, page 29
Planishing, page 28
Filing, page 15
Polishing, page 44
Forging, page 23
Soldering, page 35

WHAT YOU DO
Forming & Sinking the Base

1 Use the compass to mark a 3-inch (7.6 cm) circle on the 3 x 3-inch (7.6 x 7.6 cm) sterling silver square. Cut out the circle with the jeweler's saw. Center and mark a 2-inch (5 cm) circle inside the 3-inch (7.6 cm) silver disk. Place the disk on the sandbag with the marked line facing up. Using the sinking hammer, hit the marked line all the way around the disk to create an elevated lip for the base of the bud vase that's approximately ¼ inch (6 mm) high.

2 Use a file to carve and curve the edges of the 2-inch-diameter (5 cm) wood dowel into a nice gentle slope, or use a gently sloping mushroom stake if you have one. (You'll use this dowel or stake with the planishing hammer to tidy up the sinking.) Put the dowel or stake in the vise, with the curved end facing up. Rest the sunk silver disk on the edge of the dowel or stake with its elevated lip facing down. As shown in photo 1, hit the disk with the planishing hammer to give the lip a uniform slope. Place the disk on a level surface to see if it rests flat. If the disk doesn't sit properly, follow the troubleshooting steps on page 72.

3 If there's a small compass divot marking the 2-inch (5 cm) inner circle of the base, keep it intact. This mark will be helpful later. Use the files to smooth and clean the edges of the disk, making sure it remains round. Use the polishing lathe or flexible shaft with a stitched muslin wheel and tripoli compound to polish the disk. This partial polishing will help with cleaning later.

Shaping the Tapered Tube

4 Use the scribe to mark a centerline down the length of the 4½ x 2-inch (11.4 x 5 cm) sterling silver sheet. Mark two points near the corners of one end of the sheet, each ⅛ inch (3 mm) in from the edge. Draw two slightly arched lines down the length of the sheet, each starting at the corner of the unmarked ends and ending at the ⅛-inch (3 mm) mark on the same edge of the sheet (see figure 1). Use the saw to cut down this line, creating a tapered edge for the tube of the bud vase.

5 Place the tapered silver strip on the sandbag or on the block with the U- or V-shape channel. Use the narrow forging hammer to hit along the centerline of the metal. It immediately will start to fold. Slightly turn the metal, and, again, hit along its length. Turn the metal, this time in the opposite direction, and hammer again. The silver should begin turning into a tapered tube. Continue turning and hammering until you can no longer get the forging hammer into the tube.

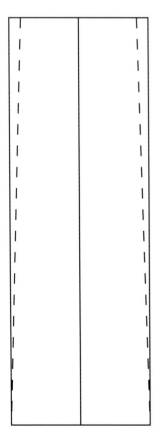

figure 1

Connecting the Tube Edges

6 Rest the tube on the U- or V-channel hammering block. Use the planishing hammer to hit the metal from the outside, pushing the tube edges closer together. You may not be able to get the edges perfectly lined up. As long as some of them meet cleanly without overlapping, you'll be able to tack-solder the seam with a simple butt joint as shown in photo 2. (Tack-soldering a few points on the tube seam will anneal it. Annealing the silver will make the remaining tube edges come together more easily.) If you happen to overlap an edge, stick a narrow dowel into the tube and push the edges open. Use a planishing hammer or a rawhide or wooden mallet to retap the edges and make them flush. (Overlapping edges will never appear smooth, no matter how much they're cleaned and polished.) Use binding wire to stabilize the position of the tube if you wish, and then hard-solder its seam. Remove all binding wire. Pickle the tube. Rinse and dry it completely.

Shaping the Tube

7 Use the files to remove excess solder and solder marks. Place the tube on the ½-inch (1.3 cm) steel dowel, and tap it with the planishing hammer or a rawhide or wooden mallet to make it round. Keep in mind that hitting the tube in one area more than another will stretch and flare that area out. Use the planishing hammer to exaggerate the gentle cone shape of the tube if you like.

8 Use the files to clean the ends of the tube until they're flat. (The form should stand straight when rested on its narrow end.) Attach a stitched muslin wheel to the polishing lathe or flexible shaft. Polish the cone-shape tube with tripoli compound to remove all file marks and scratches, and remove as much firescale as possible. (Cleaning individual parts before they're connected is always a good idea. It makes future polishing and finishing faster and easier.)

Soldering the Base & Tube

9 Mark a 10-mm circle at the center of the sunken disk (the base of the vase), approximating the diameter of the narrow end of the tube. Flux the base and the tube, and prepare to solder. For this connection, solder in the pallion style as shown in photo 3, using medium or easy solder. (The pallion method helps ensure that you don't use too much solder or

LOOK AT A NEW SILVER PIECE YOU'VE MADE AND ASK YOURSELF
A FEW QUESTIONS. DO YOU LIKE IT? IS IT WHAT YOU WANTED?
WHAT DON'T YOU LIKE ABOUT IT? IS THE FINISH GOOD? WHAT
WOULD YOU DO DIFFERENTLY? HOW WOULD YOU ACHIEVE
WHAT YOU WANT? ALL OF THESE ARE GOOD QUESTIONS, AND
THEY WILL HELP YOU GROW AS A SILVERSMITH.

THE PROJECTS

72

produce clumps of solder in areas that are difficult to reach and clean.) As you heat the base and the tube, carefully watch them to make sure the solder doesn't melt and jump from one piece to the other. The solder should flow and attach the two pieces. It's extremely important that all excess solder be removed from this seam without removing any metal, so work as cleanly as possible. I cannot stress this enough!

10 Make certain the vase is watertight; fill it with water and put some sawdust or a paper towel in the sunken base. If the dust or towel gets wet, there's a leak. Find it and fill it with solder as needed before you continue. Let the fully soldered bud vase cool. Pickle, rinse, and dry it.

Polishing the Vase

11 Attach a stitched muslin wheel to the lathe and polish the bud vase with the tripoli compound to remove firescale. Polish carefully, especially in hard-to-reach areas. Figure out how best to hold the vase in order to clean its corners. Most importantly, take your time and remain alert. Rinse the bud vase with hot water. Clean your polishing area and store the tripoli supplies.

12 Attach a stitched muslin wheel to the lathe and carefully polish the bud vase with the white diamond compound. Rinse the vase in hot soapy water. Clean your polishing area and store the white diamond supplies.

13 Attach a stitched muslin wheel (and one clean balloon wheel if possible) to the lathe, and polish the vase with rouge compound. If you're working on a double-arbor lathe, as you polish the vase, quickly brush it against the clean balloon wheel to remove any streaking compound. When the vase is completely polished, a final buffing against a clean balloon wheel will give it a bright final sheen. Rinse in hot soapy water and pat the vase dry.

Variation

The design of a bud vase can grow and change for many reasons. This project features a gentle cone shape that you can exaggerate to suit your style and individual needs. Consider the size and type of flower that you want the vase to hold. A long-stemmed rose requires a vase with a wide base and a tall container; whereas you can display a few pansies in a vase with a narrow base and a small container.

Troubleshooting: Creating a Flat Base

1 Rest the base upside down on its raised lip. Is it sitting flat all the way around the edge of the lip? If not, the base isn't even.

2 Rest the base right side up and see if it rocks. If the area within the 2-inch (5 cm) inner circle isn't flat, the base will rock. To eliminate this, put the base on a metal hammering surface, and tap it with the planishing hammer. (Use a rawhide mallet if you wish. It will leave fewer marks, but it will take more time). As you hammer, the inner circle of metal will start to bow up toward the hammer. This elevates the center of the base, allowing the outer base edges to act as a new support.

3 Turn over the base. Are the lip edges now flush? If not, use your hands to twist the base and correct the edges.

4 Place the base right side up again. Is it sitting flat? If not, sink it a tiny bit more to stretch the metal more uniformly. If the lip of the base is uniform and the base doesn't sit flat, it's unevenly stretched, and must be adjusted.

5 If minor balance problems still exist, make the base sit flush and file the lip edges until they're flat and level.

Hair Comb

Fashion a glamorous hair accessory from sterling silver sheet and wire,
and embellish it with a pierced motif or a planished surface if you're so inspired.

WHAT YOU NEED

Materials
Sterling silver sheet, 18 gauge,
   3½ x 1½ inches (8.9 x 3.8 cm)
Sterling silver wire, 16 gauge,
   9 inches (22.9 cm) long
Sterling silver wire, 16 gauge,
   3 inches (7.6 cm) long
Hard and easy solder

Hammers
Rawhide or wooden mallet,
   for step 3, option A
Planishing hammer
Chasing hammer,
   for step 3, option C

Other Tools
Scribe
Jeweler's saw and saw blades
Files
Needle files
Sandbag, dapping block, or large
   mushroom stake, for step 3,
   option A
Mushroom stake, large dap, or
   sinking hammer, for step 3,
   option B
Center punch, for step 3, option C
Drill bits, for step 3, option C
Swage block or anvil

Kits
Soldering kit, page 47
Polishing kit, page 47

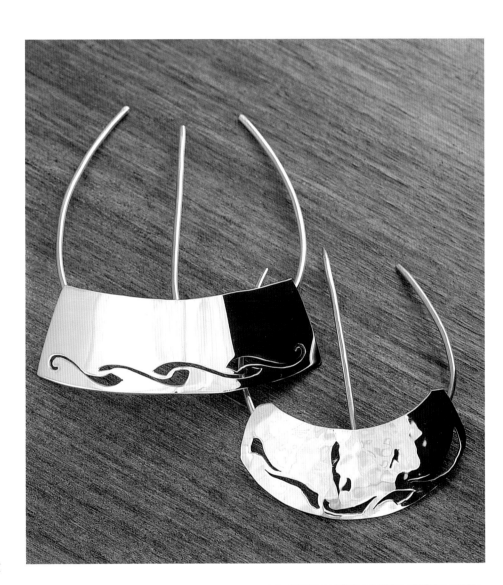

Techniques
Sawing, page 12
Filing, page 15
Planishing, page 28
Piercing, page 13, for step 3, option C
Soldering, page 35
Polishing, page 44

Before You Begin
This project has three *tines*, or rods,
that hold the comb in the hair. Its
design works especially well in thick
hair. To hold fine or thin hair, you may
want to make a comb with more tines.

LINE D   LINE D

LINE A

LINE C

LINE B

LINE E   *figure 1*   LINE E

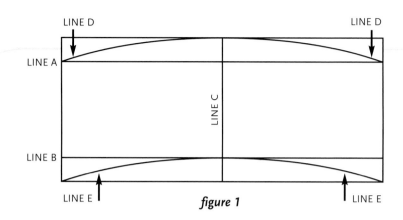

WHAT YOU DO

Creating the Comb Form

1 Measure and mark a line lengthwise across the 3 ½ x 1 ½-inch (8.9 x 3.8 cm) sterling silver rectangle that's ¼ inch (6 mm) down from its top edge (figure 1, line A). Measure and mark a second line lengthwise across the silver, ¼ inch (6 mm) up from its bottom edge (figure 1, line B). Measure and mark a centered third line across the width of the silver and perpendicular to the first two lines (figure 1, line C). Using a felt-tip pen or a scribe, draw an arch, starting at the left edge on line A, proceeding to the point where line C intersects with the top edge of the silver, and then back down to line A on the right silver edge (figure 1, line D). This is the top arch of the comb. From the lower left corner of the silver, mark a matching arch to the intersection of lines B and C, and then back down to the lower right corner of the silver (figure 1, line E). Use the jeweler's saw to cut out the shape of the comb (lines D and E).

2 File the cut edges of the silver, removing any marks, burrs, or uneven saw lines. Round the outer edges of the comb if you like. (It's much more difficult to do this later when the comb is completely shaped and soldered.)

Fashioning the Comb Surface

3 You have three options for your comb's surface.

Option A

If you want to create a smooth comb with a mirror finish, use the rawhide mallet to gently bend the silver into a nice flattering curve. Bend in the outer edges about ¼ to ½ inch (6 to 13 mm) from the centerpoint of the comb. Make this bend by holding the silver at an angle and using the mallet to give it the curve, by hammering the silver on a sandbag or into a shallow cavity in a dapping block, or even by hand (see photo 1). You can also make the bend from the outside of the piece on a large mushroom stake. Use whatever method you're most comfortable with or whatever tool is most handy.

Option B

If you want a planished texture on the hair comb, use a mushroom stake. Any size will do. The smallest mushroom is the most versatile. (If you don't have a mushroom stake, clamp a large dap or even a sinking hammer in a vise.) Planish the silver surface while creating its gentle curve. Be careful not to try to match the curve of the stake; you only should use it as a hammering surface.

Option C

If you want to pierce the surface of the comb to create decorative patterns, now is the best time. Since the middle of the arch of the comb will be backed with the sterling wire and there will be wire extending down from the center of the comb, you don't want to pierce these locations. I recommend piercing the top of the comb. Draw the pattern on the silver with a fine-point felt-tip pen. Drill and saw out the pierced design.

Constructing the Comb Tines

4 Lightly planish the 16-gauge sterling silver wires with the planishing hammer. Don't try to shrink or draw out the metal; just give it a nice texture. (Hair comb tines with a bit of texture hold hair better than those with a mirror finish.)

5 Hard-solder the 3-inch-long (7.6 cm) piece of sterling silver wire perpendicular to the centerpoint of the 9-inch-long (22.9 cm) wire as shown in photo 2. The result will look like a T with an extra-long top. Pickle, rinse, and dry the tines.

6 Bend each end of the 9-inch (22.9 cm) wire toward the center and the 3-inch (7.6 cm) tine. (The wire should look a little like a pitchfork.) Make the widest part of the structure, from outer tine to outer tine, approximately 2¾ inches (7 cm) apart. This measurement is also the approximate height of the tines.

Attaching the Tines to the Comb

7 Rest the tines across the middle of the back side of the comb with their ends facing down. Use your hands to gently bend the tine base to match the curve of the comb. Prepare to solder these two surfaces. (I recommend using easy solder. Since you're creating a seam that's visible only to the user, the color of the solder isn't important. Also, you won't have to worry about the middle tine releasing under the heat of the soldering torch.) Center and solder the tines to the back side of the comb. Solder about 2 inches (5 cm) of the tines to the comb, 1 inch (2.5 cm) on each side of the middle tine. The outside edges of the tines don't need to be attached. This mobility allows the comb wearer to extend the end tines as needed to a more suitable length for holding the hair.

Cleaning & Polishing the Hair Comb

8 File and clean the back side of the hair comb and tine ends so they won't grab and break the wearer's hair. Attach a stitched muslin wheel to the polishing lathe and gently clean and polish the tines with tripoli compound. As shown in photo 3, always polish in the direction of the tines. Never move them against or across the wheel. (You may find it easier to polish the back side of the comb with a looser wheel. Just remember that the tines can become caught in the polishing machine in an instant, so remain alert.) Clean the comb's front side and remove all firescale. Wash the comb in hot soapy water and dry it. Clean your polishing area and store the tripoli supplies.

9 Prepare the polishing lathe with a stitched muslin wheel and white diamond compound. Be very mindful of the tines as you polish the hair comb. Only polish the front face of the comb. (I don't recommend polishing the tines beyond the white diamond compound. The shinier and smoother they are, the less secure they hold the hair.) Rinse the hair comb in hot soapy water. Clean your polishing area and store the white diamond supplies.

10 I recommend polishing the surface of the comb all the way to the rouge level. The brighter the shine, the prettier the comb will look in someone's hair. The exposed surface isn't large or complex, so definitely take the polishing process as far as possible. Attach a stitched muslin wheel (and one clean balloon wheel if possible) to the lathe, and polish the comb with rouge compound. If you're working on a double-arbor lathe, as you polish the comb, quickly brush it against the clean balloon wheel to remove any streaking compound. When the comb is completely polished, a final buffing against a clean balloon wheel will give it a bright final sheen. Rinse in hot soapy water, and pat the comb dry.

Variation

Feel free to alter this design, changing its proportions or the height of its arch in a manner you find becoming. This gentle arch or one slightly more exaggerated works very well with the overall form and function of the piece and nicely crowns the hair.

Condiment Dish

This condiment dish, also known as a porringer, *is a popular and versatile form. Leave its handle solid and you'll have a wonderful location for traditional engraving, or pierce and saw the handle with a decorative cutout design.*

WHAT YOU NEED

Materials

Sterling silver disk, 18 gauge,
    5½ inches (13.9 cm) in diameter
Sterling silver sheet, 18 gauge,
    2 x 4 inches (5 x 10.2 cm)
Photocopied handle template, page 156
Hard solder

Hammers

Sinking hammer
Planishing hammer
Rawhide or wooden mallet

Other Tools

Compass
Sandbag, dapping block, or carved
    wood block
Mushroom stake
Files
Needle files
Wood dowel, 2 inches (5 cm) in
    diameter (optional)

Vise (optional)
Swage block or anvil (optional)
Sandpaper or emery cloth
Jeweler's saw and saw blades

Kits

Soldering kit, page 47
Polishing kit, page 47

Techniques

Sinking, page 29
Planishing, page 28
Filing, page 15
Transferring designs, page 10
Sawing, page 12
Soldering, page 35
Polishing, page 44

WHAT YOU DO

Sinking the Bowl

1 Anneal the sterling silver disk. Pickle, rinse, and dry it. Place the compass on the disk's centerpoint, and mark five concentric circles on its surface, each ½ inch (1.3 cm) apart.

2 Place the marked disk on the sandbag, dapping block, or carved wood block, holding it at a 30- to 45-degree angle as shown in figure 1. Beginning at the largest circle mark, use the sinking hammer to sink the silver disk. Hit the marked line all the way around the disk, making sure to hit the metal where it has room to move rather than where it's in contact with the hammering surface (see figure 2). Move in to the next marked line and repeat. Continue sinking the disk

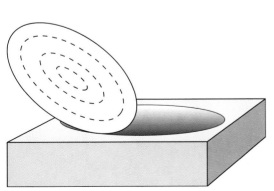

figure 1

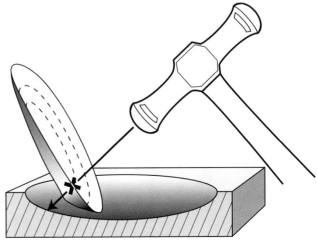

figure 2

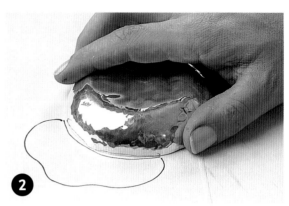

until its base is approximately 1 inch (2.5 cm) deeper than its lip, forming a nice shallow bowl. (You may have to sink the disk more than once to achieve the proper depth. If so, remember to re-anneal the silver between turns.)

Planishing the Bowl

3 Draw a set of concentric circles on the bottom side of the sunken disk, each ½ inch (1.3 cm) apart. Place the disk on the mushroom stake. Locate the circle mark with the 2½-inch (6.4 cm) diameter, and planish around this line (see photo 1). Your goals are to pull up the edges to create a consistent curve, to form a uniform bowl, and to remove undesirable sinking marks. Take your time and hammer with precision. More hammering on one side of the bowl than the other can create an uneven depth and lip, so planish with care. Planish more than once if needed. This bowl will not be easy to planish after the handle is attached.

Checking If the Bowl Is Round & True

4 Use a compass to draw a circle with a 5½-inch (13.9 cm) diameter on a sheet of paper. Place the bowl upside down on top of the drawing and check if the shapes match. If the drawing is larger than the bowl, make smaller circles on other pieces of paper until you create a template you can use as a guide. Adjust the contour of the bowl as needed with a planishing hammer or a rawhide or wooden mallet to fit the drawing. Use a file to smooth the edges of the bowl, and then recheck that it's round and true.

5 If the bottom of the bowl doesn't sit flat, now is the time to fix it. File and sand off the edges of the 2-inch-diameter (5 cm) wood dowel. Grip the dowel in the vise and place the sunken bowl on top. Use the planishing hammer to hit against the bowl's gentle curve, evening its lower edge. Don't hit below the bottom of the curve. Flip the bowl over, and place it right side up on a swage block or anvil. Holding it flat to the surface, hit inside the bowl, in the middle of its base with the planishing hammer. Make only a few careful strokes. This will cause the bottom surface to slightly bow inward, and it should sit flat.

6 Tape the sandpaper or emery cloth to a flat surface. Place the bowl, lip side down, on the paper and carefully rub the bowl back and forth. Continue this process as long as needed until all edges are uniform.

Creating the Handle

7 Rest the lip of the bowl over the corresponding curve of the photocopied handle template (see photo 2). Make sure these curves closely match. (Since the handle will be soldered to the bowl, the curves should match as much as possible to reduce cleaning.) Transfer the photocopied handle template onto the 18-gauge, 2 x 4-inch (5 x 10.2 cm) sterling silver sheet. Use the jeweler's saw to cut out the handle pattern. Use files to clean the cut edges of the handle.

3

Soldering & Cleaning the Handle & Bowl

8 Flux the inside of the bowl and the underside of the handle. Rest the handle face down on the soldering station. Position the bowl, lip side down, on the handle. Make sure these two parts completely meet. Hard-solder the handle even with the edge of the bowl or on top of it (see photo 3). Let the dish air-cool, and then pickle it. (Take your time with the pickle. Larger pieces have a greater surface area on which the acid must be allowed to work.) Rinse and dry the dish.

9 Use a file, needle file, or a square stick covered with sandpaper to clean the solder seams and make the edges flush. If the solder clumped, bled, or jumped underneath the bowl, remove it now. Check the bowl's top side to see if the solder bled through. If so, file it off. If you soldered the handle on top of the edge of the bowl, the handle may stick over it. File off any overhang. If you soldered the handle even to the bowl's edge, the edges may be irregular. File them level.

Polishing the Condiment Dish

10 Attach a stitched muslin wheel to the lathe and polish the dish with tripoli compound. (If you don't mind removing some of the planishing hammer marks, you can start with an abrasive wheel. It will remove firescale more quickly, but it also will remove hammer marks more thoroughly.) Pay special attention inside the bowl of the dish. To safely polish this area, you'll need wheels that are 4 inches (10.2 cm) or smaller. Also, since the mouth of this dish isn't very large, always keep a careful watch on the dish edges while polishing. Search for any traces of firescale, especially on the soldered edge. You can use stiffer wheels to reach the seams and remove the firescale. Rinse the dish, wash it in hot soapy water, and dry it. Clean your polishing area and store the tripoli supplies.

11 Attach a stitched muslin wheel to the lathe and polish the dish with white diamond compound. Since the edges of the handle and bowl were smoothed earlier with the tripoli compound, they'll require less work now. Check the dish for firescale. Rinse the piece, wash it in hot soapy water, and let dry. Clean your polishing area and store the white diamond supplies.

12 Attach a stitched muslin wheel (and one clean balloon wheel if possible) to the lathe, and polish the dish with rouge compound. If you're working on a double-arbor lathe, as you polish the dish, quickly brush it against the clean balloon wheel to remove any streaking compound. When the dish is completely polished, a final buffing against a clean balloon wheel will give it a bright final sheen. Rinse it in hot soapy water and pat the dish dry.

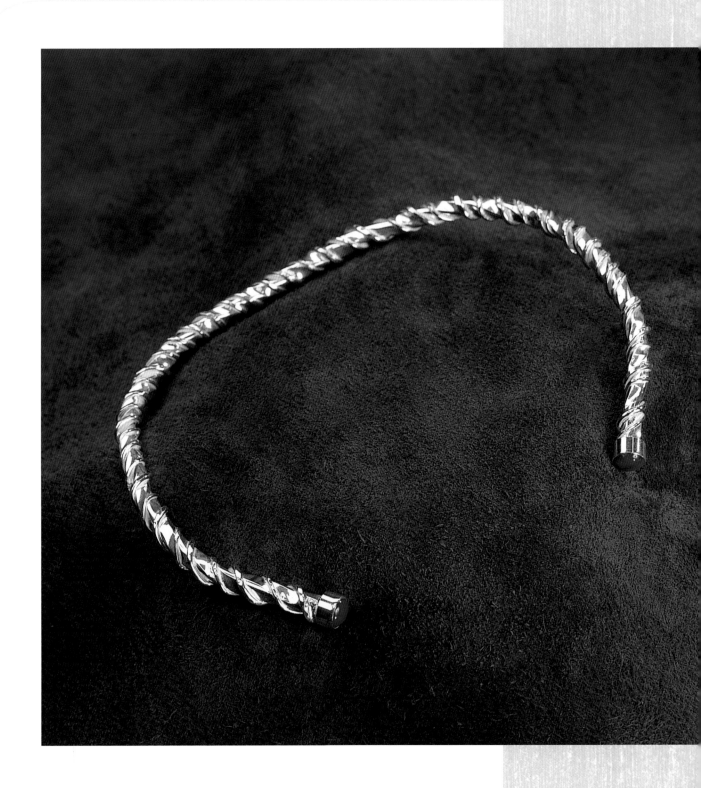

Torque Necklace

The end caps on a torque face the front of the wearer and are ideal places for ornamentation.
Ancient torques were often capped with cast animal figures or crystals.

WHAT YOU NEED

Materials

Sterling silver rod, 1 gauge,
    12 inches (30.5 cm) long
Hard, medium, and easy solder
Sterling silver wire, 18 gauge,
    24 inches (60.9 cm) long
Sterling silver wire, 12 gauge,
    24 inches (60.9 cm) long
2 pieces sterling silver bezel wire,
    26 gauge, each 1 1/16 inches
    (2.7 cm) long
2 pieces scrap silver, 18 gauge, each large
    enough to cover a bezel back
2 cabochon stones of your choice,
    each 8 mm

Hammers

Forging hammer
Rawhide or wooden mallet

Tools

Swage block or anvil
Vise
Clamp grips or pliers
T-stake
Files

Needle files
Tweezers or third arm (optional)
Sandpaper (optional)
Burnisher

Kits

Soldering kit, page 47
Polishing kit, page 47

Techniques

Forging, page 23
Soldering, page 35
Filing, page 15
Polishing, page 44

WHAT YOU DO

Wrapping & Soldering the Wires to the Rod

1 Place the 12-inch (30.5 cm) sterling silver rod on the swage block or anvil. Use the forging hammer to hammer the rod square and stretch its length to 13 inches (33 cm). Using hard solder, connect one end of both the 18-gauge and the 12-gauge wires to one end of the hammered square rod. Place the soldered end of the rod into the vise. Wrap the wires up and around the length of the rod. As shown in photo 1, medium-solder the loose wire ends to the unsoldered rod end. Pickle, rinse, and dry the wire-wrapped rod.

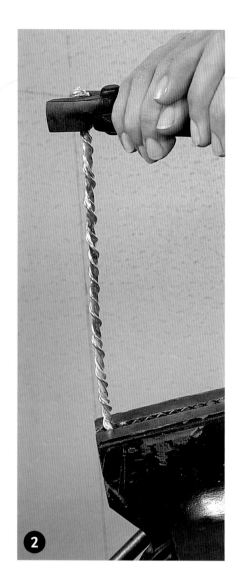

2 Place one end of the wire-wrapped and soldered rod into the vise. Using the clamp grips or pliers, begin twisting the rod in the same direction as the soldered wires (see photo 2). Twist the rod until all of the wire is taut against its surface. Release the rod from the vise, take it to the soldering station, and easy-solder the wire to the rod to ensure a strong and stable connection. Pickle the soldered rod. Rinse and let dry. Place one end of the wire-wrapped and soldered rod in the vise. Twist the rod until you're satisfied with its appearance and remove it.

Shaping the Torque

3 Use your hands to bend the rod around the edge of a sturdy table, and then use a rawhide mallet and a T-stake to complete the torque's half-round curve. (Since the torque is essentially a cuff for the neck, its opening needs to be large enough to fit onto the neck, but round enough to securely rest on the shoulders.)

Making the Bezel Cups & Soldering Them to the Torque

4 Bend one sterling silver bezel wire into a circle, and connect the short ends with hard solder. Repeat for the second bezel wire. Pickle both bezels and let them dry. Use the files to clean up the bezels and make them true round. Check the bezels against the cabochon stones to make sure they are a good fit. Rest one round bezel on each of the two

scrap silver pieces. Flux and hard-solder these elements together to make the two cups to hold the stones. Pickle, rinse, and clean the cups. Cut and file off any excess silver on the back of the bezel cups.

5 Using tweezers, a third arm, or any other tool for balance and support, rest the bezel cups on the ends of the torque. (You may only want to position one cup at a time.) Center and solder the bezel cups to the torque ends with easy or medium solder as shown in photo 3. (I recommend using lower temperature solder because you're soldering something big, the torque, to something small, the bezel cups, and you shouldn't risk melting the smaller element.) Once both bezel cups are soldered to the torque, pickle, rinse, and dry it.

6 Use the needle files to make sure all soldered areas on the torque are clean and smooth. (You don't want to have worked on all that twisting and shaping to have it lost in a mess of solder!) Change to a less abrasive surface, such as a cutting wheel, a polishing wheel, or even a felt wheel with tripoli compound, and use the flexible shaft to clean the torque.

Polishing the Torque

Before You Begin

• Be alert, use control, and be careful. A torque is the type of item a large polishing machine can easily grab from your hands. If you're not completely comfortable with the lathe, polish with a flexible shaft.

• Be gentle when polishing the torque. As you polish, you're removing layers of metal, and this could cause you to lose detail. Large polishing wheels can remove or reduce the appearance of the twisted wires, softening their lines and transforming the look of the piece.

• Be especially gentle when you polish close to the bezel cups so you don't cut through the metal. Just clean the cups enough make the solder seams invisible.

7 Attach a stitched muslin wheel to the polishing machine of your choice, and carefully polish the torque with tripoli compound. Rinse the torque, wash it with soapy water, and let dry. Clean your polishing area and store the tripoli supplies.

Left: bezel cup with lip that's too tall
Right: bezel cup with lip at correct height

8 Attach a stitched muslin wheel to the lathe, and carefully polish the torque with the white diamond compound. Rinse the torque in hot soapy water. Clean your polishing area and store the white diamond supplies.

9 Rest the torque on your neck or on that of a friend to see if it needs further shaping. Does the back of the torque arch down enough to support the front and keep the ends resting on the collar bone? Does the torque sit evenly? Readjust the shape of the torque as needed. You may want to rest it on a flat surface to make sure all the arcs and curves of the necklace are uniform and balanced.

Setting the Cabochon Stones

10 Place one stone into one bezel cup. Check if the lip of the cup is too tall for the stone. (The edge of the cup should line up slightly past the point where the stone begins its curve to the top [see photo 4]. The cup should secure the stone without blocking its beauty.) If the cup is too tall, use sandpaper to remove the excess metal. Starting at the 12 o'clock position, use the burnisher to gently push the bezel cup in around the edge of the stone. Next burnish the stone at 6 o'clock, then 3 o'clock, and, finally, 9 o'clock. These four burnished points will hold the stone in place. Slowly and carefully push the remaining metal edge around the stone.

Finishing the Torque

11 Attach a stitched muslin wheel to the polishing machine of your choice, and carefully polish the torque with the rouge compound. Rinse the torque, wash it with soapy water, and pat-dry. Try on the torque and check for any uncomfortable burrs or rubbing points. If any exist, burnish, polish, or file them off.

Curio Container

Small decorative containers make storage more beautiful, especially when they're polished sterling silver.

WHAT YOU NEED

Materials
Sterling silver sheet, 18 gauge,
   7 x 2 inches (17.8 x 5 cm)
Hard, medium, and easy solder
2 sterling silver disks, 18 gauge,
   each 2½ inches (6.4 cm) in diameter
Sterling silver wire, flat or bezel,
   24 gauge, 7 inches (17.8 cm) long,
   approximately ⅖ inch (1 cm) wide

Hammers
Rawhide or wooden mallet
Sinking hammer
Planishing hammer

Other Tools
Files
T-stake
Compass
Jeweler's saw and saw blades
Dapping block, carved cavity,
   or sandbag
Sandpaper
Needle files
Burnisher (optional)
Steel wool

Kits
Soldering kit, page 47
Polishing kit, page 47

Techniques
Soldering, page 35
Filing, page 15
Sawing, page 12
Sinking, page 29
Planishing, page 28
Polishing, page 44

WHAT YOU DO
Forming the Container Shape

1 Bend the short ends of the 7 x 2-inch (17.8 x 5 cm) sterling silver sheet into a large tube. Hard-solder together the 2-inch (5 cm) ends. I recommend soldering from the outside to make the seam easier to clean. All sides, inside and out, will be visible on the finished piece, so it's very important to solder a good, pitless seam. Let the silver tube cool, and then quench and pickle it. Use the files to clean off any excess solder.

2 Place the soldered silver tube on the T-stake. Use the rawhide or wooden mallet to hammer the tube perfectly round. Draw a circle with a 2¼-inch (5.7 cm) diameter on a piece of paper or board and check both edges of the tube against it.

3 Determine one edge of the tube to use as the base of the container. Hard-solder one 2½-inch (6.4 cm) silver disk onto the base, making sure the seam is clean, pitless, and secure. (I recommend soldering from the outside. Cleaning the inside of any container is always more difficult than cleaning and filing from the outside.) Let the piece cool, and then pickle it.

4 Rinse all the pickle off the soldered piece, dry it, and then fill it with water to check for any holes in the seam. If holes exist, fill them with solder now. Take the solidly soldered piece to your bench and use a jeweler's saw to cut off all excess silver from around the base of the container. File the cut edges smooth.

STERLING WORDS

USE MY TECHNIQUES AS GUIDELINES, BUT ALLOW YOURSELF THE FREEDOM TO EXPLORE WITHIN THESE GUIDELINES. YOU MAY FIND A DIFFERENT METHOD THAT WORKS BETTER FOR YOU AND STILL ACCOMPLISHES THE SAME GOALS.

Cutting the Lid's Lip

5 Mark the container ⅖ inch (1 cm) down from its opening. This is the lid's lip. Place the container on the bench pin. Use a jeweler's saw to cut through three places on this line, rotating the container to evenly cut along the entire piece as shown in photo 1. Don't cut through the entire container, but mark and cut deep into the ring at the 12 o'clock, the 4 o'clock, and the 8 o'clock positions. Cut as deep as you can without removing the upper lip section. Keeping the lip on the base ensures that the base and the lid of the curio container will match. (If you cut the lip free now and solder it to the lid later, there's no guarantee that the pieces will fit.) These cuts are also breathing holes for the next solder, so you can work on the piece without stressing the metal and without risking a blow out or implosion.

Creating & Attaching the Lid's Domed Disk

6 Use the sinking hammer and a dapping block, cavity, or sandbag to dome the top surface of the container and give it the appropriate curve. Sink the second 18-gauge sterling silver disk so it has a 3/16 to ⅖-inch (.5 to 1 cm) rise at its centerpoint. The highest point of the dome must be in the center of the disk. To help evenly sink and stretch the metal, you may want to scribe or mark the metal at ¼-inch (6 mm) increments.

7 Planish the sunken disk to remove any lumps. If you used a dapping block or a carved cavity, you may not need to

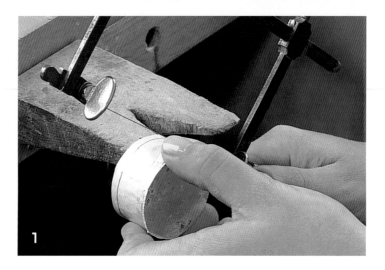

planish, but you probably will if you used a sandbag. (When used with a sandbag, sinking hammers leave more defined marks.) Planish on top of the rounded surface of a T-stake. If your T-stake doesn't have a rounded surface, you can planish on a small mushroom stake or even a sinking hammer secured in a vise.

8 Hard-solder the domed disk to the top of the container. As you heat the work, remember that the container is a much bigger piece of metal than the disk. Rest the disk upside down, place the container within its edge, and solder. This upside-down style of soldering is much easier for this project. It enables you to see what the solder is doing and where it's going at all times. Let the container air-cool, and then pickle, rinse, and dry it.

Detaching the Lid

9 Using the jeweler's saw to finish cutting off the lip of the lid is really tricky. The metal will probably fight you, but just follow the grooves you made in step 5. Cut all the way around the lid until it separates from the base. If there's any remaining flux or residue, put the container back in the pickle for a few min-

utes. Rinse, and let dry. If there's a ledge on the top of the container, cut it off and file the cut edge smooth.

Forming & Attaching the Container's Inner Lip

10 Use the 7-inch (17.8 cm) length of 24-gauge sterling silver wire to construct the inner lip of the curio container. The wire will be formed into a ring that fits within the container, but first you must determine its proper length. Measure the width of the metal at the container's edge. Multiply this figure by two or three. Trim this length off the end of the wire. (If you trim off a bit more, the wire will still work, but if you don't trim enough, the wire won't fit within the container.) Hard-solder the two wire ends together. Cool, pickle, rinse, and dry the wire.

11 Sand the edges of the container and its lid completely flat. Use a needle file to remove a tiny bit of metal inside the edges of both the container and the lid. Check the two parts against each other, making sure they're both sanded and filed completely smooth. (Once you attach the lip to the container, you won't easily be able to work on this edge.)

12 Check the soldered wire ring against the opening in the top of the container. If the ring is too big, use the jeweler's saw to cut it down, and then re-solder and re-check it. If the ring is a little bit small, lightly planish it on the T-stake. This hammering stretches the metal, so constantly check to make sure you don't make the inner ring too large for the lid. Once these two elements fit together snugly, they can be soldered. Leave about 3 mm of the ring sticking out past the edge of the lid. Solder the ring to the lid with medium or easy solder as shown in photo 2. Remember how thin and small the ring is, and make sure not to melt it as you attach it to the lid. Let the piece cool, and then pickle it. Rinse and dry the lid.

Fitting the Lid & Container

13 Use needle files to clean any lumpy or visible solder off the lid. The connection of the lid and its inner lip should be as clean, invisible, and square as possible. Filing the lid may take time, but be patient. A clean connection lets the container close properly.

14 Place the lid on the base of the container and check to see if these two elements fit. It may be a snug connection. Polishing the container will make this connection easier, but you may need to lightly file the inside lip area of the base of the container. Alternately, you could gently tap in the lid lip with a hammer, creating a slight curve (see photo 3), or you could burnish the inside of the container, smoothing the surface where the lip rests when the container is closed. Simply rub the burnisher against the surface of the base interior. This technique takes time and can be mind-numbing, but it does a good job if you give it the chance. (Hint: have some good music playing or something exciting to think about.)

Polishing the Container

15 Place a stitched cotton or muslin wheel on the polishing lathe and prepare it with tripoli compound. Clean, polish, and buff the container. Remove file marks and firescale. (There will be a lot of firescale on this piece, but, since it's a simple form, it shouldn't be too difficult for you to remove.) Take your time and remain alert. Rinse the container in hot soapy water and let dry. Clean the polishing station and store the tripoli supplies.

16 Attach a stitched cotton wheel to the polishing lathe and prepare it with the white diamond compound. Repeat step 15, polishing the top and bottom of the container with the white diamond compound. Rinse the container in hot soapy water, and let dry. Clean the polishing station and store the white diamond supplies.

17 Scrub the inside of the container with soapy water and steel wool. This step creates a nice interior surface and allows the container to look completely finished and functional without additional polishing or sanding.

18 Attach a stitched muslin wheel to the polishing lathe and prepare it with the rouge compound. Give the top and bottom of the container a final polish.

Variations

You can create an oval curio container using these same techniques. I encourage you to explore the possibilities of shape and form. In order to make square or angled containers, however, you'll need to learn a few more techniques not covered here.

Stone-Capped Baby Rattle

A handmade baby rattle makes an unforgettable gift, and its silver orb cools a teething baby's gums.

WHAT YOU NEED

Materials

Sterling silver sheet, 18 gauge,
   2 x 4½ inches (5 x 11.4 cm)
Sterling silver bezel wire, 26 gauge,
   1⅙ inches (2.7 cm)
Sterling silver bezel wire, 26 gauge,
   ⅞ inch (2.2 cm)
Hard, medium, and easy solder
Sterling silver sheet, 20 gauge,
   2¼ x 1³⁄₁₆ inches (5.7 x 3 cm)
Cabochon stone of your choice, 8 mm

Hammers

Forging hammer
Planishing hammer
Rawhide or wooden mallet
Sinking hammer
Chasing hammer
Small sinking hammer

Other Tools

Compass
Jeweler's saw and saw blades
Swage block or anvil
Wood block (optional)
Dowel, 8 mm in diameter
Binding wire
Pliers
Files
Tapered round dowel or sanded wood
   dowel, ⅓ inch (8 mm) in diameter
Large dap or mushroom stake
Sandpaper
Center punch

Drill bits
Small daps, approximately ⅕ to
   ⅓ inch (5 to 8 mm)
Needle files
Burnisher
Soft cotton rag or leather chamois

Kits

Soldering kit, page 47
Polishing kit, page 47

Techniques

Sawing, page 12
Soldering, page 35
Forging, page 23
Planishing, page 28
Sinking, page 29
Filing, page 15
Polishing, page 44

Before You Begin

For this project, you'll sink two silver half-spheres of equal proportions. You can sink silver with much more control in a dap cavity than in a sandbag. If you don't have a dapping block yet, I recommend carving a half-sphere cavity into a wood block before you begin. Make the cavity about 1 inch (2.5 cm) deep and ¾ inch (1.9 cm) in diameter.

WHAT YOU DO

Preparing the Silver

1 Use the compass to mark two circles on the 2 x 4½-inch (5 x 11.4 cm) 18-gauge sterling silver sheet, each 2 inches (5 cm) in diameter. Use the jeweler's saw to cut out both circles. This leaves a 2 x ½-inch (5 x 1.3 cm) silver sheet. Use the compass to mark and the saw to cut out four ½-inch (1.3 cm) disks from the remaining silver.

2 One at a time, bend and then hard-solder both pieces of the sterling silver bezel wire into small tubes. (If the bezel wire is cut slightly shorter than the measurement on the materials list, you can stretch the soldered tube. It's much harder to shrink the tube than to stretch it.) Use a file to clean the tubes, removing all solder bumps and dimples. Place the two bezel wire tubes aside.

Making the Tube for the Rattle Handle

3 Mark a centerline down the length of the 2¼-inch-long (5.7 cm) piece of 20-gauge sterling silver. Place the marked silver on top of a V- or U-shaped channel in the swage block or wooden block. (You can also screw or nail a small wood piece into your workbench and hammer into the edge of the newly created "V.")

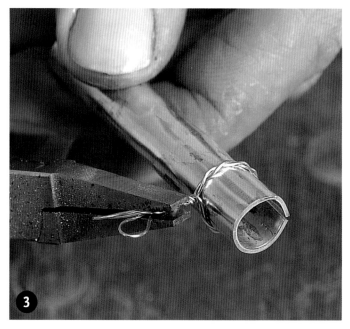

THE PROJECTS

4 Use the forging hammer to hit the metal down the marked line. The metal will start to bend. Hit the metal again, this time between the centerline and the edges, on both sides as shown in photo 1. With repeated hammering, the edges will begin to close in on themselves, and you'll no longer be able to hit inside the metal.

5 Hammer the outside of the metal with the forging hammer to bring together the edges of the silver sheet (see photo 2). If at any point the sheet doesn't appear to be forming a tube, place the wooden dowel inside the bent silver. Use the planishing hammer or the rawhide mallet to hit the silver and correct its shape. You may have to anneal the silver in order to accomplish this.

6 Tap the sides of the silver tube with the rawhide mallet or hit the tube edges with the forging hammer to bring them close enough for soldering. Don't worry if the form slightly changes from true round; you can tap it back into shape after soldering.

7 Cut at least three 3-inch (7.6 cm) pieces of the binding wire. Wrap the wire in a few locations down the length of the tube. Use the pliers to twist the ends of the binding wire and pull together the tube edges as shown in photo 3.

8 Hard-solder the seam of the silver tube. Remove the binding wire, and then pickle the tube. If the solder didn't flow down the entire seam on the first try, solder again until the seam is fully connected. Remove the binding wire, and pickle. Use the files to remove excess solder from the seam.

9 Thread the wooden dowel down the center of the soldered tube. Use the rawhide mallet and/or the planishing hammer to correct the tube shape as needed. Hammer the tube's high points, while leaving its low points alone. Rock the tube around and keep hammering until the tube is true to round. This is the rattle's handle. (If making the rattle for a younger baby, you can cut the handle shorter if desired.)

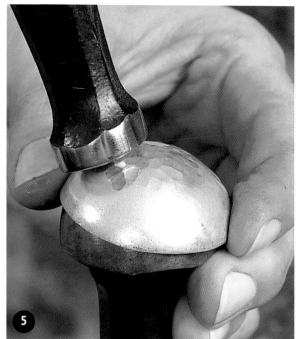

Forming the Bezel Cup for the Cabochon Stone

10 Place one small silver bezel wire tube on a small wooden dowel or tapered dowel. Gently hammer the tube with the rawhide mallet to make it round. Repeat with the second wire bezel tube. Check the bezel against the cabochon stone to make sure it is a good fit. The smaller tube should just fit into the larger one, leaving a 1-mm external lip. Starting from the bottom of the bezel cup, use medium solder to attach the two tubes in this position, leaving the upper lip slightly raised and clean for the stone setting (see photo 4).

Creating Two Domes for the Rattle Ball

11 Place one 2-inch (5 cm) sterling silver disk on the dapping block or carved wood block. Use the sinking hammer to sink the disk to a depth of at least 1⅛ inches (2.9 cm), making it a dome. Repeat this step to sink the second 2-inch (5 cm) disk.

12 Place one dome created in step 11 over a large dap, a mushroom stake, or a sinking hammer gripped in a vise. As shown in photo 5, use the planishing hammer to remove any surface irregularities in the silver. Repeat this process on the second dome. You should have two fairly evenly matched domes.

13 Tape a piece of sandpaper to your workbench. Rest one dome on the sandpaper, and gently push it back and forth until its edges are flat and level (see photo 6). Sand the edges of the second dome. Bring together the edges of the two domes to see if they match. Continue carefully sanding the dome edges as needed until they fit perfectly.

14 Mark and dimple the centerpoint of one dome. Use a ⅛- to ¼-inch (3 to 6 mm) bit to drill a breathing hole at the dimpled mark. (This hole ensures that no pressure builds up in the rattle when it's soldered. It also permits any residual flux, acid, and polishing compounds to be rinsed out of the rattle.)

7

Making the Beads for the Rattle Ball

15 Use a small sinking hammer to sink each of the four ½-inch (1.3 cm) silver disks into domes. (It's easiest to sink the domes into a dapping block with daps, but you can also use a small sinking hammer and a sandbag. Accuracy is not as important when doming these disks.) Sand the dome edges following the method described in step 13. Mark and dimple the centerpoint of all of the domes. Use a 1-mm bit to drill a hole at the dimpled marks. Hard-solder the four domes into two beads, making sure each bead has a drilled hole. (Don't be concerned with the beauty of these beads. They're going inside the rattle.) Pickle and rinse the soldered beads. Let dry.

Connecting the Elements to Form the Rattle

16 Rest the small silver beads inside the matching large domes. Flux the edges of the domes and rest them together, making sure the beads are inside. As shown in photo 7, medium-solder the entire seam without pits, holes, or cavities. (Be careful not to generate enough heat to flow the solder on the beads. This would stop them from making noise inside the rattle.) Let the sphere cool. Pickle and rinse.

17 Place the bezel cup, outer lip up, into one end of the rattle handle, leaving 2 mm of the lip above the handle. Use medium solder to attach the bezel cup to the handle. Pickle, rinse, and let dry.

18 Rest the rattle ball on the solder station with its drilled hole facing up. Flux the area around the hole. Flux the rattle handle end that isn't attached to the bezel cup. Balance the handle on the ball over the drilled breathing hole. Use easy solder to connect the handle to the ball. (Keep in mind that you need to heat the whole object. If you only heat the area you're soldering, you run the risk of burning or melting that area and not getting a clean attachment.) Once the handle and ball are soldered, let the rattle cool, and then pickle. Thoroughly rinse the inside of the rattle and hang it with the handle facing down to drain all fluids. Rinse and drain the rattle again. Let it dry.

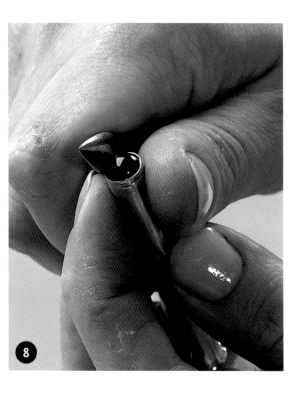

8

STERLING WORDS

PREPARE TO GET DIRTY EVERY
TIME YOU USE POLISHING
COMPOUNDS. TRIPOLI DUST
FLIES. WHITE DIAMOND DUST
FLIES MORE. ROUGE DUST
FLIES THE MOST.

93

THE PROJECTS

Filing & Polishing the Baby Rattle

19 Beginning with a medium file, remove excess solder from all surfaces. File the solder off the rattle ball seam and off the connection between the handle and the ball. File excess solder off the bezel cup if needed. Repeat this process using finer files. Where the edges need to be very clean and crisp, use needle files to finish removing surplus solder.

20 Attach a stitched muslin wheel to the polishing lathe. Polish the rattle with the tripoli compound. Take your time and remove all firescale. In doing so, you're also likely to remove any extra file or scratch marks. Polish with added care on the edges and at the bezel cup. You don't want to lose the rattle's clean edges or remove too much metal from the bezel

cup. Rinse the rattle in hot water with liquid dishwashing soap. Clean your polishing area and store the tripoli supplies.

21 Using a stitched muslin wheel attached to the polishing lathe, carefully and thoroughly polish the rattle with the white diamond compound. Clean the rattle with soap, rinse it with hot water, and let dry with the handle facing down to drain all liquids. Clean your polishing area and store the white diamond supplies.

Setting the Cabochon Stone & Finishing the Rattle

22 Rest the 8-mm cabochon stone inside the bezel cup on the rattle handle. Starting at the 12 o'clock position, use the burnisher to gently push the external cup around the edge of the stone as shown in photo 8. Push the bezel at 6 o'clock, then 3 o'clock, and, finally, 9 o'clock. These four burnished points hold the stone in place. Slowly and carefully push the remaining bezel cup edge around the stone.

23 Attach a balloon muslin wheel to the polishing lathe. Gently polish the baby rattle to its highest shine with rouge compound. Rinse the rattle with hot water and liquid dishwashing soap. Pat the rattle dry with a very soft cotton rag or a leather chamois.

Forged Fork & Spoon

It may be hard to believe, but you can actually forge functional and well-designed cutlery out of straight silver rods.

WHAT YOU NEED

Materials

2 sterling silver rods, 1 gauge, each 6 inches (15.2 cm) long

Hammers

Forging hammer
Planishing hammer
Sinking hammer
Rawhide or wooden mallet

Other Tools

Swage block or anvil
Jeweler's saw and saw blades
Needle files
Dapping block, carved wood block, or sandbag
Dowel or curved surface (optional)

Kits

Soldering kit, page 47
Polishing kit, page 47

Techniques

Forging, page 23
Sawing, page 12
Planishing, page 28
Filing, page 15
Sinking, page 29
Polishing, page 44

WHAT YOU DO

Forging the Neck & Handle of the Fork & Spoon

1 Use a felt-tip pen to mark each of the sterling silver rods 1½ inches (3.8 cm) from one end. (One area from the marked line to the rod end will be the bowl of the spoon, and one will be the face of the fork. The rod area beyond the marked lines will be the handles.)

2 Rest one rod on the swage block or anvil with the line marked in step 1 on the edge and the 1½-inch (3.8 cm) length extending past it. Use the forging hammer to hit the rod at the marked line *squarely*. This means to hit the metal with the length of the hammer face perpendicular to the length of the rod. This striking position moves the metal up and down, not side to side, allowing for the lengthening and the tapering of the rod. Once you forge the rod on one side, turn the rod over 90 degrees and squarely hammer the side of the metal not yet extended. (Because you're stressing the silver in this process, you'll need to anneal the rod between turns.) The swage block or anvil will pressure the other side of the rod, and, as you continue to forge, the rod will start to taper and to turn square, forming the neck of the cutlery piece (see photo 1). Follow this method to forge the rod from 7.4 mm square to 4 mm square. Repeat this step to make the neck on the second rod.

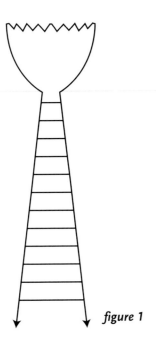

figure 1

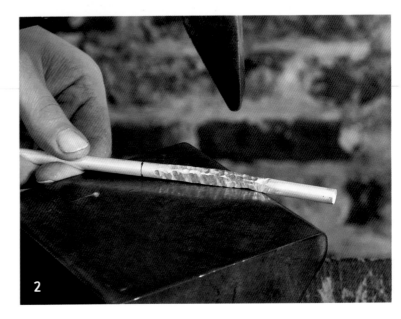

3 Measure and mark a point 2½ inches (6.4 cm) up the handle from the neck. This is the middle of the handle. Beginning at the neck on one rod, use the forging hammer to slowly flare and taper the silver back out to the full width of the rod (see photo 2 and figure 1). Repeat this process to taper the second rod from the neck to the middle of the handle.

4 Decide which rod to use as the spoon and which to use as the fork. To shape the bowl of the spoon and face of the fork, you'll use the forging hammer to move the width of the metal below the neck. (You've previously moved the length of the metal.) As shown in photo 3 and figure 2, hit the silver with the hammer face running parallel to the length of the silver rod. The metal may fight you at first, but as you begin to push the metal, it will flatten, stretch wider, and become easier to hit. Anneal the silver as needed. Stretch the face of the fork to 1 inch (2.5 cm) wide and the bowl of the spoon to 1½ inches (3.8 cm) wide. The ends of the cutlery pieces should look like they're beginning to take form.

5 With its face running parallel to the length of the rod, use the forging hammer to uniformly flare the handles. Forge one centerline down the length of the handle. Forge a row below, and then a row above the centerline, extending these rows 3½ inches (8.9 cm) from the neck (see photo 4). Repeat this sequence several times. (If the hammer blows are uneven, the handle will begin to bend. Should this happen, turn over the handle and hammer the row opposite the one that caused the bend.) As shown in figure 3, lightly forge the back end of the handle to meet the tapered front end at the 3½-inch (8.9 cm) mark.

Shaping the Bowl of the Spoon

6 Use the jeweler's saw and files to shape the spoon bowl into an oval. Create a contour with clean edges.

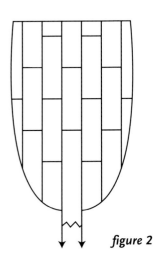

figure 2

Planishing the Fork & Spoon

7 Planish the neck of the spoon and fork to remove the rough forging hammer marks and ensure a nice, clean-looking piece. If the pieces are a bit lopsided or unevenly flared, reshape them now. Use a hammer to even out the flare (a forging hammer for more movement, a planishing hammer for less) and/or a file to make the edges more uniform.

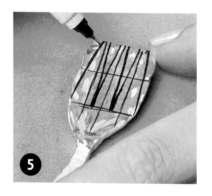

figure 3

Sinking the Bowl of the Spoon

8 Use the sinking hammer and a dapping block, a carved wood block, or a sandbag to sink the spoon bowl to approximately ¼ to ½ inch (.6 to 1.3 cm) deep at its lowest point. Hit the silver evenly to make a uniform bowl. Once the proper depth is achieved, carefully file the spoon bowl edges so they flare out equally, and then gently clean its surface. Pause often to check that you're not overfiling the bowl. As you work, frequently lift the spoon about an arm's length away from you and look at its face and back side to see if it's uniform from the middle to both edges.

Creating the Tines & Bending the Fork

9 Use a planishing hammer to planish the entire face of the fork. To determine the placement of the fork tines, mark a line approximately two-thirds of the way up from the end of the face. Mark a centerline down the length of the face of the fork. Divide each side of the centerline in half, and mark the length of the fork face. You'll have four equal sections and three marked lines which will be used to make the tines. Make a mark 1 mm away from each side of each marked tine guideline. As shown in photo 5, these new lines, six in all, are the cutting lines. Use the jeweler's saw to carefully cut around these lines to create the tines (see photo 6).

10 Use the rawhide or wooden mallet to bend the fork to the appropriate angle over a dowel, the edge of a table, or a curved surface. (When the fork rests flat, the ends of the tines should match the depth of the spoon, approximately ¼ to ½ inch [.6 to 1.3 cm] off the table.) Carefully file and clean the edges of the fork. Repeatedly check your work to make sure you don't take away too much metal.

Polishing the Fork & the Spoon

Before You Begin

• The face of the fork is its most fragile area. The cuts and tines are thin, and they can easily be bent out of shape. Support the face against the polishing wheel and always polish in the direction of the tines. Polishing across the tines increases the risk of the machine grabbing the fork, which could damage your hard work and be dangerous.

• The larger polishing wheels won't reach into the bowl of the spoon. You'll take care of this area later with a flexible shaft and a small polishing wheel.

• If you want the polishing to go faster and you aren't overly concerned with keeping the forged hammer marks on the fork and spoon, you can start cleaning with an abrasive wheel or a pumice wheel. These tools remove firescale much more quickly, but they also remove forging marks and metal. If you choose to use abrasive wheels, always work slowly and cautiously.

11 Attach a stitched cotton or muslin wheel to the polishing lathe. Apply the tripoli compound to the wheel. Clean the surfaces of the fork and the spoon, removing all firescale. Polish the edges of the fork and spoon, smoothing away any file marks and making the pieces nice to look at and to handle. Take all the time you need at this stage, and be sure to take breaks. Rinse the polished fork and spoon, and wash them with hot soapy water. Clean your polishing area and store the tripoli supplies.

12 Attach a stitched cotton or muslin wheel to the polishing lathe. Load the wheel with white diamond compound, and polish the fork and spoon. Rinse the polished fork and spoon, and wash them with hot soapy water.

13 Attach a small stitched muslin wheel to the flexible shaft. Polish the inside of the spoon bowl with tripoli compound. Remove all firescale from the inside of the bowl, rinse the spoon, and then continue polishing the fork and spoon on the lathe with white diamond compound. Rinse the polished fork and spoon, and wash them with hot soapy water. Clean your polishing area and store the white diamond supplies.

14 Place a balloon cotton or muslin wheel on the lathe, load it with rouge compound, and give a final polish to the fork and spoon. Rinse the silver pieces, and then wash them with hot soapy water.

Pedestal Bowl

You'll sharpen your sinking and planishing skills as you hammer out this exquisite bowl.

WHAT YOU NEED

Materials
Sterling silver disk, 18 gauge,
    7 inches (17.8 cm) in diameter
Sterling silver sheet or rod, 18 gauge,
    ¼ x 6 inches (.6 x 15.2 cm)
Hard solder

Hammers
Sinking hammer
Planishing hammer

Other Tools
Compass
Dapping block, sandbag, or carved
    wood block
T-stake or mushroom stake
Circle template, 6 inches (15.2 cm)
    in diameter
Emery paper or sandpaper
Files
Needle files
Kitchen scrub, abrasive cleanser,
    or steel wool (optional)

Kits
Soldering kit, page 47
Polishing kit, page 47

Techniques
Sinking, page 29
Planishing, page 28
Soldering, page 35
Filing, page 15
Polishing, page 44

WHAT YOU DO
Sinking the Disk

1 Anneal, and then cool the 7-inch (17.8 cm) sterling silver disk. Pickle, rinse, and dry it. Use the compass to mark concentric circles on the top of the disk, each ½ inch (1.3 cm) apart.

2 Place the silver disk on the dapping block, sandbag, or carved wooden block with the marked circles facing up. Hold the metal at a 30- to 45-degree angle to the surface. Use the sinking hammer to hit the outer edge of the disk and move the metal down. (The edge will slightly curl up and wrinkle, but don't worry. You're pushing and hollowing out the metal.) Continue to hammer all the way around the disk, creating a uniform sunken area equidistant from its edge. This is your first "turn." As shown in photo 1, hammer a second "turn" at the same angle, using the sinking hammer to hit the disk just inside the first sunken area. Repeat this process in concentric circles to sink the entire disk, a "full turn."

There should be a recognizable curve to the bowl at this point, although it is probably uneven and lumpy.

3 To make a more uniform and smoother bowl, rest it on the jeweler's bench or a flat work surface. Without increasing the bowl's angle, use a sinking hammer to tap down the high areas to match the sunken areas, but no farther (see photo 2). Hammer with less force than you used to sink the disk. You don't need to keep the bowl on any curve or angle; hitting directly onto the wood is good. At this point, you aren't stretching the metal anymore. You're simply creating a more uniform surface prior to annealing and prior to its next "full turn." Anneal the bowl and let it cool. Pickle, rinse, and dry the bowl.

4 Look for the concentric circles marked on the bowl in step 1. Retrace the circles with a felt-tip pen, or, if they're no longer visible, draw new ones. Following the process described in steps 2 and 3, use the sinking hammer and the dapping block, sandbag, or carved wood block to sink and smooth the bowl again. Remember to keep the metal in a dapping cavity that's deeper than the curve of the bowl or to keep it turned up at an angle, such as 35 to 45 degrees, that allows the hammer to force the metal to stretch. After completely sinking and smoothing the bowl a second time, re-anneal it. Sink and smooth more as needed. Once you create the desired angle on the outer edge of the bowl, stop hammering that area and start sinking the interior of the bowl. (When sinking a bowl, its center and base will always need the most stretching and hammering.) Anneal the bowl and let it cool. Pickle, rinse, and dry.

Planishing the Bowl

5 Use a compass to draw concentric circles on the exterior of the bowl, each ½ inch (1.3 cm) apart. Rest the interior of the bowl on the mushroom or T-stake. Starting on the innermost marked circle, use the planishing hammer to planish the exterior of the bowl in concentric circles, working outward toward its edge (see photo 3). Wherever you hammer, always position the bowl flat on the stake. This gives you a planishing surface that minimizes the movement of the metal. (At this stage, you're not forcing the metal in any direction, stretching it in order to sink the bowl, or expanding the volume of the form. Your goal here is to work on the bowl's overall surface and contour, bringing it uniformity and symmetry through planishing.) The bowl should start to take on a faceted surface.

6 Planish the entire bowl again, following the marked circles from the center to the outer edges. As you hammer, rotate the bowl in the opposite direction of your previous "full turn." This helps ensure a well-balanced and round bowl, prevents any spiraling hammer marks, and develops hammer control. Anneal the bowl and let it cool. Pickle, rinse, dry, and then planish again. I strongly recommend re-marking the concentric circles on the exterior of the bowl after each annealing and before each round of planishing. This extra step helps you find the center of the bowl and maintains uniformity. Don't anneal the bowl after planishing it the last time.

7 Place the bowl upside down on top of the circle template to check that it's round. If not, now is the time to fix it. Place the bowl upside down on top of a flat surface and see if its edges sit flush. If not, rest the bowl edges down on a sanding surface. Gently rub the bowl back and forth until its edges are even and its lip is true and clean. Recheck the bowl against the circle template to make sure it stayed round during sanding.

Creating & Attaching the Bowl's Ring Base

8 Bend the 6-inch (15.2 cm) sheet or rod of 18-gauge sterling silver into a circle. Hard-solder together the ends of the circle. Cool, pickle, and rinse the circle. File off any excess solder. Place the circle on the T-stake or the mushroom stake. Hammer it into a round form and flare out one edge as shown in photo 4. The circle should have a narrow edge and a wide edge like a sideways V. Planish the circle to match the surface of the shallow bowl.

9 Place the bowl, bottom side up, on the soldering station. Make sure you can see a marked centerpoint on its base. Center the narrow edge of the silver circle on the base of the bowl. (The wide edge will provide more stability as the base.) Flux the circle and the bowl, and prepare to solder. Use hard solder, in pallion or stick form, to attach the base ring

to the bowl as shown in photo 5. (Since you're soldering together two pieces of dramatically different sizes, be careful where and how much you heat the metal. You don't want to melt the base ring.) Try to be as neat and tidy as possible with the solder. The cleaner the soldering, the less filing you'll have to do later. Let the piece cool, and then pickle, rinse, and dry it. Check the solder seam to make sure it flowed over the entire ring. Re-solder any areas that were missed.

10 Use the files to remove any excess solder from the seam of the base and the bowl. Use large files to remove deep areas of solder or needle files if there isn't much to clean. Use a flexible shaft with an abrasive wheel attachment to clean off any solder inside the base ring. Sand the seam to remove as many file marks as possible.

Polishing the Bowl

11 Place a stitched muslin wheel on the polishing lathe. (Use one larger and one smaller wheel on a double-arbor lathe, if possible.) Prepare the wheel with tripoli compound. Polish the edge of the bowl to remove any remaining sanding marks, being careful not to let the edges catch in the wheel. Polish the interior of the bowl, the most difficult surface to clean, with the tripoli compound. There will be a lot of firescale, so this step will take time. (You can use a more abrasive wheel, but remember that it will more quickly and easily remove decorative hammer marks.) Be gentle and remain alert during this first stage of polishing to keep the faceted texture of the planishing hammer and only remove the firescale. Always keep the bowl moving, rotating it back and forth and rocking as you polish. Even when you want to con

centrate on just one area, rock back and forth over and around that area, to create a uniform surface.

12 Polish the exterior of the bowl with tripoli compound to remove all firescale. Work around the base ring. Whenever possible, hold the bowl at an angle to polish inside the edge of the ring. (If the stitched muslin wheel isn't small enough to reach inside the ring, use a flexible shaft with a muslin wheel and tripoli compound.) Rinse the bowl in hot soapy water and pat dry. Clean your polishing area and store the tripoli supplies.

13 Attach one stitched muslin wheel (and one balloon wheel if your machine has two arbors) to the lathe. Prepare the wheel with white diamond compound, and polish the interior of the bowl. Double check for firescale, and, if there is any left that isn't removable with white diamond compound, mark it with a felt-tip pen and continue to polish the bowl. If there is no firescale, polish the inside of the bowl with the balloon wheel for a higher white-diamond shine. Repeat this step to polish the exterior of the bowl. When cleaning the exterior, always be aware of the top and base edges, and stay alert so they won't catch in the lathe.

14 Examine the bowl and mark any remaining firescale with a felt-tip pen. Repeat steps 11 to 13 to repolish the marked areas. When switching back and forth between tripoli and white diamond, always clean the polishing area and store the wheels and compounds to prevent contamination.

15 Attach a balloon wheel to the lathe, load it with rouge compound, and polish the bowl. When finished, buff the bowl with a clean balloon wheel to reduce streaking.

Variation

If the bowl interior is too bright and shiny for your taste, you can easily give it a brushed or scratched surface. Simply use a common household item, such as a kitchen scrub, an abrasive cleaning agent, or steel wool to transform the finish. This intentional "distressing" can be a good thing, since the interior of the bowl will receive the most use. Giving the bowl interior a light texture helps disguise the wear marks that would stand out on a highly shined surface.

STERLING WORDS

USUALLY, IF YOU SPOT FIRESCALE IN ONE AREA, IT WILL LIKELY BE IN OTHERS.

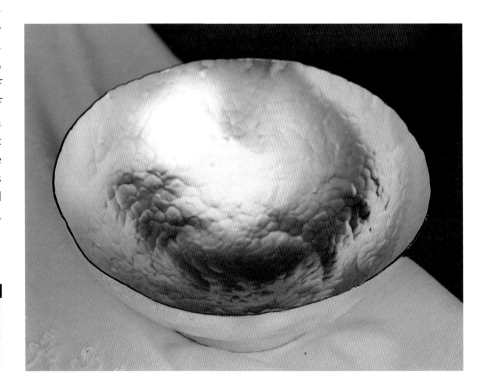

Baby Cup

Create a silver heirloom for a special baby by soldering a tube, base, and handle, and then planishing or simply polishing the fabricated form.

WHAT YOU NEED

Materials

Sterling silver sheet, 18 gauge,
   3 x 6 inches (7.6 x 15.2 cm)
Hard, medium, and easy solder
Sterling silver disk, 18 gauge,
   2¼ inches (5.7 cm) in diameter
Sterling silver sheet, 18 gauge,
   ²⁄₅ x 4 inches (1 x 10.2 cm)

Hammers

Rawhide or wooden mallet
Planishing hammer
Forging hammer (optional)

Other Tools

Pliers
Narrow T-stake, approximately 1 to
   1¾ inches (2.5 to 4.4 cm) wide
Binding wire
Files

Needle files
Compass
Sandpaper
Jeweler's saw and saw blades
Large wooden dowel
Abrasive pad or steel wool (optional)
Cotton or leather strips, 1 inch
      (2.5 cm) wide, at least 18 inches
      (45.7 cm) long

Kits

Soldering kit, page 47
Polishing kit, page 47

Techniques

Soldering, page 35
Filing, page 15
Planishing, page 28
Sawing, page 12
Polishing, page 44

STERLING WORDS

WHATEVER WAY YOU SOLDER, THERE IS BOUND
TO BE A SEAM THAT NEEDS CLEANING, AND CLEAN-
ING IS TEDIOUS WORK. AS YOUR SOLDERING SKILLS
IMPROVE, YOU'LL NEED TO CLEAN LESS AND IT WILL
TAKE LESS TIME. IN THE MEANTIME, DON'T FORGET
TO GET UP OUT OF YOUR SEAT ONCE IN AWHILE.
LOOK ACROSS YOUR YARD OR YOUR STREET.
SWING YOUR ARMS. TAKE A BREATHER.

WHAT YOU DO

Constructing the Tube

1 Bend the 3 x 6-inch (7.6 x 15.2 cm) sterling sheet into a tube. (If bending the metal with your hands or with pliers is difficult for you, use a rawhide or wooden mallet and a T-stake.) Make sure when they meet that the two 3-inch-long (7.6 cm) ends butt up against each other and their corners are level. Use binding wire as needed to secure the tube in this position.

2 Flux and hard-solder the tube seam completely shut. For the solder to flow, you'll need to heat the entire seam area. However, since you don't want the solder to "jump" all over the seam, try not to flux beyond the soldering area, and make sure you uniformly heat the entire tube. Solder from the outside, using the heat to pull the solder in and through the tube seam. Let the tube air-cool. Remove any binding wire. Rinse, pickle, rinse, and completely dry the tube.

3 File off any excess solder from the outside of the tube. If the tube isn't round enough for you to easily access its interior with a file, gently tap it into shape with a rawhide or wooden mallet. Use files, needle files, or a flexible shaft with abrasive wheels to remove excess solder from inside the tube. Remove all cleaning marks on the inside of the tube.

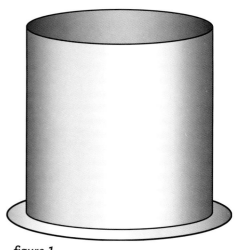

figure 1

Planishing the Tube

4 Rest the soldered tube on the narrow T-stake and begin to planish. Hammer in any comfortable pattern, but keep your strokes uniform throughout the entire process to create a symmetrical cup. Begin planishing on one end of the tube and slowly work your way around its circumference. As shown in photo 1, gradually "climb" the length of the tube, hammering one turn after another, until the whole form is planished. If you closely follow this process, the tube will automatically try to sit in a true round form. If it doesn't, anneal the tube and planish again, making more uniform hammer strokes. You can also rest the tube on a wooden bench and use the rawhide or wooden mallet to push the tube in one direction or another.

5 Use the compass to draw a circle with a 2-inch (5 cm) diameter on a scrap piece of paper. Rest the tube on the circle and see how well it fits. If the tube is larger or smaller, draw a second circle that conforms to its size. Use this drawing as a template to ensure the tube is true round. If it isn't, keep shaping the tube with a planishing hammer, a rawhide or wooden mallet, or your hands.

6 Make sure the tube edges sit flat on a level surface. To do this, rest the tube on end and check for any points of light between the surface and the end of the tube. If light is visible, secure a piece of sandpaper to a rigid surface with tape. Place the tube on the paper and sand its edges flat. After sanding, recheck the tube against the circle template to make sure it hasn't been knocked out of true round.

Soldering the Base to the Tube

7 This step takes time and a fair amount of heat. Make sure to flux well and evenly heat the large tube and the small 2¼-inch (5.7 cm) sterling silver disk. (I even keep spray flux handy and apply more as needed.) Using hard solder is preferable, but medium solder is acceptable for this connection. You can solder this seam from above with the cup on top of the disk (see figure 1), or from below with the disk above the cup (see figure 2). You may only be able to tack-solder the disk to the tube on the first pass. (If you form a complete seam on the first try, congratulate yourself and move on to step 8.) Solder what you can, and, when the flux is burned off or the metal has moved in an uncontrollable way, turn off the torch, and let the metal cool. Pickle, rinse, dry, and prepare to make a second pass with the solder.

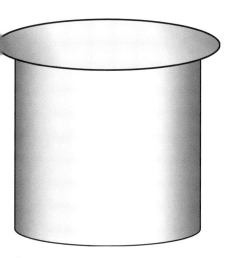

2

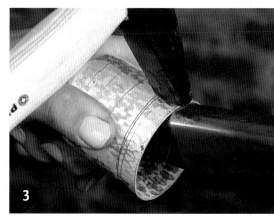

3

figure 2

Hint: If you weren't able to solder the entire seam on the first try, the disk may have shifted and pulled away from the tube. If so, use a mallet to tap the disk down onto the tube. Once the surfaces are flush, solder again. This time around, you may want to switch to a medium solder. (If you started with medium solder, stick with it, but don't use easy solder for this seam. It will be used later to attach the handle.) To fully attach the disk, it may take more than one, or even two attempts with the torch.

8 Pickle, rinse, and dry the fully soldered form. Use the jeweler's saw to cut off any silver from the disk that extends beyond the tube. File off all excess solder until the base of the cup is clean and round. To remove any burrs that may have formed when cleaning up the cup, run the file over the outer edge of the base.

9 Pour some water into the cup, place it on a dry surface, and watch for any leaks. If there's a leak, mark its location with a felt-tip pen. Flux the marked areas on the inside and the outside of the cup. Resolder the cup from the outside for easier cleaning. Use the heat of the torch to pull the solder through the leaking hole. Cool the cup. Pickle, rinse, and dry it. Use files to remove all excess solder from the cup, and recheck for leaks. Continue this process until the cup is watertight.

Shaping the Cup

10 If the cup doesn't sit flat, carve a centered, shallow, round cavity in the end of a large wooden dowel. Gently tap and push the middle of the base of the cup into the cavity or use a metal dowel as shown in photo 2. With its base tapped inward, the cup will sit flat on its edges and be more stable.

11 If you want to further shape the cup, such as curving its base or flaring its lip, do so now. These alterations are much simpler to accomplish before the handle is attached. To curve the cup base, use the same wooden or metal dowel used in step 10, but hit the edges of the base, not its center. To flare the cup lip, gently rest it on the T-stake, holding the base of the cup toward you and slightly above the height of the lip. Use the planishing or the forging hammer to hit the area you want to flare (see photo 3). The forging hammer flares the lip faster, but you'll need to planish out any forging marks.

THE PROJECTS

4

Creating & Attaching the Handle

12 Place the ⅖ x 4-inch (10.2 x 1-cm) sterling silver strip on the T-stake. Use the planishing hammer to planish the strip to match the cup. To form a slight curve or dome in the handle, planish the center of the strip more than its edges.

13 Use your hands to bend the planished silver strip over the T-stake into the desired handle shape. Re-planish it while it's in the appropriate curve. Check the handle ends against the cup and make sure they fit. The handle ends and the cup must meet cleanly for a solid attachment. File the ends of the handle as needed so they sit flush on the curved cup surface.

14 Rest the cup on its side with its soldered seam facing up. (I recommend attaching the handle on top of the seam to hide it.) Support the cup between some pumice stones or pieces of firebrick if you wish. Fully flux the solder area and attach the handle to the cup with easy solder as shown in photo 4. (Using easy solder prevents the previously soldered seams from becoming loose or melting.) Let the cup air-cool. Pickle, rinse, and dry it. File and/or sand off any burrs or excess solder.

Cleaning & Polishing the Cup

15 To clean inside the cup, you may need to make a custom tool. For example, you can glue sandpaper to the end of a wooden dowel to reach into tight areas. The easiest and most uniform way to polish the internal surface, however, is with an abrasive wheel attached to a flexible shaft, with an abrasive pad, or with steel wool. Abrasive pads and steel wool will burnish the internal surface of the cup, leaving a brushed finish. Always use them with soap and water and rinse off all residue before polishing the exterior.

16 Place a stitched muslin wheel on the polishing lathe. (Use two wheels if you have a double-arbor machine.) Prepare the wheel with tripoli compound and thoroughly polish the cup and its

5

edges, removing all firescale. (This cup needs to be child friendly. Little hands and mouths should be able to safely use it without coming in contact with burrs or surface irregularities.) Since the cup is a relatively large and heavy silver piece, be extremely careful it doesn't get caught in the polishing lathe.

17 The most difficult place to polish is under the cup handle. Here you'll need to be careful and creative. You can remove imperfections with files, and then use the flexible shaft with different abrasive and wheel attachments. Alternately, you can use a strap. This option isn't as fast as a wheel but can polish hard-to-reach areas. This can be the first and only tool you use for polishing under the

cup handle, or you can simply use it for final finishing. Nail strips of leather or cotton to your workbench. Label each strip with its corresponding polishing compound. Thread the cotton or leather strip through the cup handle and hold the loose strip end in your hand. Apply the tripoli polishing compound to the strip. Slide the cup back and forth against the surface of the strip (see photo 5). This method will offer you much more control and finesse. Rinse the cup in hot soapy water, and pat dry. Clean your polishing areas and store the tripoli supplies.

18 Attach the one stitched muslin wheel (and one balloon wheel if possible) to the lathe and polish the cup with the white diamond compound. Polish under the handle with the small wheels and/or the white diamond strip, if using. Rinse and dry the cup. Clean your polishing areas and store the white diamond supplies.

19 Attach a stitched muslin wheel (and one clean balloon wheel if possible) to the lathe, and polish the cup with rouge compound. If you're working on a double-arbor lathe, as you polish the cup, quickly brush it against the clean balloon wheel to remove any streaking compound. When the cup is completely polished, a final buffing against a clean balloon wheel will give it a bright final sheen. Rinse in hot soapy water and pat the cup dry.

Serving Pieces

This spatula and pie server both feature a phoenix-inspired design. Use my templates to replicate these patterns or create your own.

WHAT YOU NEED

Materials

Sterling silver sheet, 16 gauge,
 3 x 4 inches (7.6 x 10.2 cm) for spatula,
 or 3 x 4½ inches (7.6 x 11.4 cm)
 for pie server

Photocopied template of your choice,
 page 157

Sterling silver sheet, 20 gauge,
 1½ x 5¼ inches (3.8 x 13.3 cm)

Sterling silver sheet, 20 gauge,
 1½ x 1½ inches (3.8 x 3.8 cm)

Hard, medium, and easy solder

Sterling silver half-round wire,
 4 gauge, 4½ inches (11.4 cm)

Hammers

Chasing hammer

Forging hammer

Planishing hammer

Rawhide or wooden mallet

Other Tools

Rubber cement

Jeweler's saw and saw blades

Center punch

Drill bits

Dapping or swage block with
 V- or U-shaped channel*

Wood dowel or steel dowel or rod,
 approximately ⅜ inch (9 mm) in
 diameter (optional)

Binding wire

Pliers

Files

Needle files

Sandpaper

Leather chamois

Vise (optional)

Swage block or anvil

Cork or wood dowel, approximately
 ½ inch (1.3 cm) in diameter,
 for end cap

Kits

Soldering kit, page 47

Polishing kit, page 47

*If you don't have a V- or U-shaped channel in your dapping or swage block, you can cut one into a block of wood or use a sandbag.

Techniques

Transferring designs, page 10

Sawing, page 12

Piercing, page 13

Filing, page 15

Forging. page 23

Soldering, page 35

Planishing, page 28

Polishing, page 44

Note: These instructions are for one serving piece. Repeat the steps to make a second.

WHAT YOU DO

Making the Serving Surface

1 Use the rubber cement to adhere the photocopied template to the 16-gauge sterling silver sheet. Use the jeweler's saw to cut out the template's outer shape.

2 Use the chasing hammer and center punch to dimple inside each of the template's cutout designs. Leave enough space around the dimple so the drilled holes won't mar the edges of the design. Using a 1-mm bit, drill a hole through the silver at each dimple, and then use the jeweler's saw to cut out each of the pierced designs.

Creating the Handle

3 Mark a centerline down the length of the 20-gauge, ½ x 6¾-inch (3.8 x 17.2 cm) sterling silver sheet. Place the marked silver into the V or the U channel on the dapping or swage block. Use the forging hammer to hit the metal down the marked line. The metal will start to bend. Hit the metal again, this time between the centerline and the edges on both sides. With repeated hammering, you'll no longer be able to hit inside the metal.

4 Hammer the outside of the metal with the forging hammer to bring together the edges of the silver sheet. If at any point the sheet doesn't appear to be forming a tube shape, place the ½-inch-diameter (1.3 cm) dowel inside the silver. Use the planishing hammer or the rawhide or wooden mallet to hit the silver and correct its shape. (You may need to anneal the silver in order to accomplish this.)

5 Tap the sides of the silver tube with the mallet or hit the tube edges with the forging hammer to bring them close enough for soldering. Don't worry if the form slightly changes from true round; you can tap it back into shape after soldering.

6 Cut a minimum of three 3-inch (7.6 cm) pieces of the binding wire. Wrap the wire in a few locations down the length of the tube. Use the pliers to twist the ends of the binding wire and pull together the silver tube edges.

7 Flux and hard-solder the seam of the silver tube. Remove the binding wire and pickle the tube. If the solder didn't flow down the entire seam on the first try, don't worry. Re-bind the unsoldered areas and solder again until the seam is fully connected. Remove the binding wire, and pickle. Use the files to remove any excess solder from the tube seam.

8 If needed, thread the ⅜-inch-diameter (9 mm) dowel down the center of the soldered tube. Use the mallet or the planishing hammer to correct the shape of the tube. Tap the hammer on the tube's high points, while leaving its low points alone. Rock the tube and keep hammering its high points, until the tube is true to round. Pay special attention to both ends of the tube. Remove the dowel.

Forming the End Caps

9 Use the jeweler's saw to cut off ½ inch (1.3 cm) of the tube to make an end cap. File or sand all tube ends flat so the cap can later be attached.

10 Use the jeweler's saw to cut the 1½ x 1½-inch (3.8 cm) piece of 20-gauge silver in half. Center one end of each tube on each small silver sheet. Hard-solder together these elements to create a flat closure as shown in photo 1. Use the jeweler's saw to cut off excess silver surrounding the tubes.

Bending the Serving Surface

11 Clean the edges of the pierced serving surface with a medium file, and then with a fine file. Wrap it in a leather chamois. Place the silver in a vise or on the edge of your workbench. Position it exactly where you want the metal to bend. Gently hit the wrapped metal with the mallet to form an angle that's slightly less than 45 degrees (see photo 2).

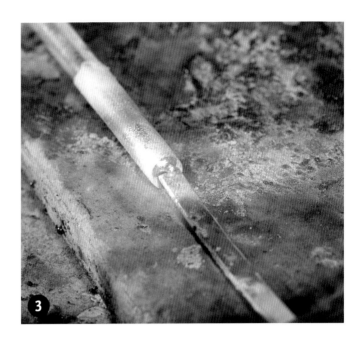

3

Soldering the Wire to the Serving Surface

12 Using the planishing hammer and the swage block or anvil, flatten one end of the 4-gauge sterling silver half-round wire into a flared shape. Clean the flattened wire end with the needle files until it's uniform and ready for soldering. Use hard solder to attach the flattened wire end in the center of the back side of the pierced serving surface.

Soldering the Wire to the Handle

13 Mark the centerpoint of the capped end of the long silver tube. This is where you'll attach the opposite end of the silver wire. Prop the tube and the wire together, making sure the pieces are centered, level, and straight. Flux both elements, and then solder them together with medium or easy solder as shown in photo 3. (Using a medium or easy solder preserves the security of the cap previously hard-soldered to the end of the tube.) Clean all the edges and seams of the service piece with the files and needle files.

Polishing the Service Piece

14 Attach a stitched muslin wheel to the polishing lathe. Apply the tripoli compound to the wheel, and polish the edges of the service piece. Be very careful not to let the wheel grab the service piece as it spins. Polish all soldered connections especially hard to remove all firescale. Carefully clean the half-round wire, gently moving it back and forth on the wheel. Whenever possible, move with the wheel instead of across it. This action is much safer. Polish the pierced silver surface. The firescale at the bend is difficult to reach, but find a comfortable way to access it and work on this area until all firescale is gone. Polish the front side and the back side of the pierced silver surface, and then the tube handle. Shine and polish the small end cap. Turn off the polishing lathe. Wash the service piece in hot water with liquid dishwashing soap to remove all of the tripoli compound. Clean your polishing area and store the tripoli supplies.

15 Attach a stitched muslin wheel to the polishing lathe. Prepare the wheel with white diamond compound. (If you have a double-arbor lathe, you may want to use a stitched wheel on one arbor and a balloon wheel on the second arbor. This flexible setup allows you easier access to the areas that need polishing.) Follow the method described in step 14 to polish all the areas of the service piece with the white diamond compound. Wash the service piece in hot water with liquid dishwashing soap to remove all of the white diamond compound. Clean your polishing area and store the white diamond supplies.

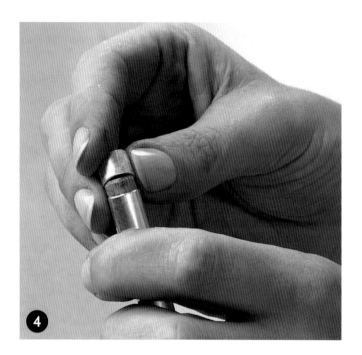

Attaching the End Cap

16 Attach a stitched muslin wheel to the polishing lathe. Prepare the wheel with rouge compound. (If you have a double-arbor lathe, you can also attach a balloon muslin wheel, but only for dusting. Don't apply any compound to the balloon wheel. Moving the silver across a clean balloon wheel will remove any streaking left by the rouge compound.) Follow the method described in step 14 to polish all the areas of the service piece with the rouge compound. Clean the service piece in hot water with liquid dishwashing soap to remove all of the rouge compound. Pat-dry the service piece with a very soft cloth. Clean your polishing area and store the rouge supplies.

17 Use the needle files and sandpaper to taper the edges of the 1/2-inch-diameter (1.3 cm) dowel or cork piece until it nearly fits into the open end of the small cap (see photo 4). Give the ends of the cork or dowel a U shape. Use the rawhide mallet to force the tapered cork or dowel into the end cap. Rest the service piece on the edge of your bench, bench pin, or vise to support its edges as much as possible. To connect the service piece with the end cap, tap it with the mallet, hitting straight down, as shown in photo 5. Polish the joint with the rouge compound to finish the piece.

Cocktail Shaker

From martinis to margaritas, every drink you make will taste better coming from this handsome, heavily hammered shaker. This advanced project requires extensive forging and planishing, so undertake it when you're ready to raise your silversmithing bar!

WHAT YOU NEED

Materials

Sterling silver sheet, 18 gauge,
   6 x 9 inches (15.2 x 22.9 cm)
Sterling silver sheet, 18 gauge,
   6 x 8⅛ inches (15.2 x 22.5 cm)
Hard solder
Sterling silver disk, 18 gauge,
   2¾ inches (7 cm) in diameter
Sterling silver disk, 18 gauge,
   2½ inches (6.4 cm) in diameter

Hammers

Rawhide or wooden mallet
Forging hammer
Planishing hammer

Other Tools

T-stake
Binding wire
Files
Sandpaper or emery cloth
Jeweler's saw and saw blades

Kits

Soldering kit, page 47
Polishing kit, page 47

Techniques

Soldering, page 35
Filing, page 15
Forging, page 23
Planishing, page 28
Sawing, page 12
Polishing, page 44

WHAT YOU DO

Bending & Soldering the Tubes

1 Using the rawhide or wooden mallet and the T-stake, bend both of the large sterling silver sheets into 6-inch-long (15.2 cm) tubes. Make the adjoining ends flat and flush. The tubes don't need to be perfectly round at this point. Use binding wire as needed to hold the tubes together. Hard-solder the seams of the silver tubes. Let the tubes cool, remove all binding wire, pickle, rinse, and dry them. Use the files to remove excess solder. Don't worry about cleaning the file marks; hammering will eliminate them.

Forging & Planishing the Bottom Shaker Vessel

2 The wider tube is the bottom shaker vessel. Use a fine-point permanent marker to draw five parallel circles around and up the length of the wide tube. Start drawing 1 inch (2.5 cm) up from either end, and space each circle 1 inch (2.5 cm) apart. These guidelines indicate your "turns" and will help you uniformly hammer the entire piece.

3 Place the marked tube on the T-stake. Using the forging hammer, hit the first marked line on the tube. (You start hammering the wide tube at this line rather than at the end in order to make it flare and taper.) Uniformly hammer all the way around the tube to make your first "turn." Hammer the second turn, hitting the tube just above the first turn and all the way around it. (The second turn falls between the first two guidelines.) As shown in photo 1, make the third turn once the second is completed. (You're now probably hammering on or close to the second marked line.) Repeat this process, working your way up the length of the tube. Remember to rest and take many breaks as you hammer. Lift your arms over your head, and periodically do something else that requires a different physical motion, such as having a cup of tea, paying your bills, or petting your dog. Come back to the hammer and complete some more turns until you forge the entire length of the tube. Stop and rest.

4 Check the hammered tube for any breaks in its solder seam (this can happen when hammering over a seam), and mark any breaks with a felt-tip pen. Starting just below the first line forged around the tube, use a planishing hammer to make a turn around the tube. The planishing hammer will smooth out the forging marks and create a more uniform surface. Planish the silver using the same method you used in step 3 to slowly and uniformly climb the length of the tube. Always remember to rest and take breaks as you planish.

5 Check the tube to see if the broken solder seam marks (if any) are still visible (see photo 2). Re-draw the marks if they've faded. Flux the marked area, and prepare to fix the seam. Anneal the entire tube, paying special attention to the marked areas. Using only hard solder, re-attach and mend the seam as shown in photo 3. Let the tube cool. Pickle, rinse, and dry it.

6 Use the fine-point marker to draw new hammering guidelines on the tube approximately ½ inch (1.3 cm) above the initial set of lines. This measurement varies from person to person due to the strength of their hammer stroke, their hammer, their aim, and their uniformity. Use the forging hammer to strike the silver on the T-stake around these lines and up the length of the tube, resting and taking breaks as needed. Once one section is fully flared, move up to the next section. You're creating an outward flare to the tube by stretching the metal with the forging hammer. You planish the tube between forging sessions to produce a greater surface area to hit and, therefore, greater surface area to move. Alternating planishing with forging also ensures a uniform surface, flare, stretch, and form. You don't absolutely have to planish the silver tube between forging sessions, but you do have to anneal it.

7 Once the tube is forged all the way to the top, planish it again. Check the tube for any solder stress cracks, and then anneal. Make all necessary solder repairs, and then cool the tube. Pickle, rinse, and dry it, and start the hammering process again. Repeat this method of forging and planishing the tube until the widest end, the top opening of the bottom shaker vessel, measures 3⅞ inches (9.8 cm) in diameter.

Note: Because there are so many variables, it's impossible to say exactly how many times you need to forge and planish the tube. Everyone has different forging and planishing hammers. You swing yours with a unique amount of strength and force. You planish differently and create your very own surface texture. I can't even predict exactly how many turns it will take me to forge and planish the tube. I may feel well, or I may feel under the weather; I may be totally focused or somewhat distracted; I may have an especially high energy level, or I might be dragging a bit—any of these factors can affect my hammer blows.

4

8 Check the flared tube against a circle template that's 3⅞ inches (9.8 cm) in diameter. It's fine if the tube is slightly inside the template. This differential will give you some room to adjust the bottom shaker vessel to fit the top. Make sure to end the hammering with a planishing turn on the bottom half of the tube, and then anneal it. This will reduce any tension in the tube prior to soldering on the base. (Under the heat of soldering, any tension left in the tube will be released, and this can make the metal move. Less tension causes less motion.) You may need to planish the entire tube more than once to remove the remaining forging hammer marks; and you shouldn't planish just one area. That would stretch just one area, throwing the tube out of shape. Anneal, measure, mark, and planish the entire surface in order to maintain the tube's true form.

(When your objective was to move and shape the metal, getting a fine and finished surface was not particularly important, but now is your chance to really work the surface. Since forging the metal into shape thinned it, it's much better to remove the hammer marks through planishing rather than through sanding and buffing. These processes take away even more metal layers.)

Soldering the Base to the Bottom Shaker Vessel

9 File and sand the 2¾-inch-diameter (7 cm) sterling silver disk as needed. As shown in photo 4, hard-solder the bottom of the tapered shaker tube to the disk. (You could use a lower temperature solder, but because hard solder most closely matches sterling silver it makes a less visible seam.) Since you're soldering together two very different size pieces of metal, be careful with the torch. You don't want to overheat and melt the disk. It could take more than one attempt to solder together these two elements. (See page 71, step 6 for a description of incremental, or tack, soldering.) Make sure, once soldered, the bottom shaker vessel is watertight and has a flat base. Let the silver cool. Pickle, rinse, and dry it. Use the jeweler's saw to cut off any excess silver from around the base. File off all excess solder.

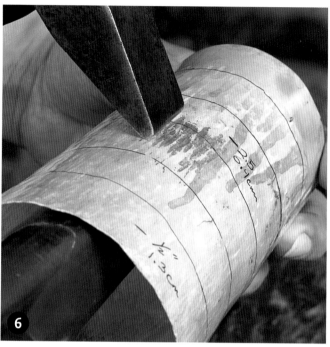

Forging & Planishing the Shaker Lid

10 Use a felt-tip pen to mark hammering guidelines on the second silver tube, the shaker lid, at 1-inch (2.5 cm) increments. The shaker lid is a completely different, yet complimentary shape to the bottom shaker vessel. The flaring of the lid doesn't begin exactly at the top, nor does it simply flare out to the base. So, to achieve this, start forging the tube on the T-stake 1½ inches (3.8 cm) in from one end as shown in photo 5. This end of the tube will be the top of the shaker lid when the two pieces are joined. Forge the lid all the way from the 1½-inch (3.8 cm) point to the bottom, annealing it between stages, until the wider end of the lid (its bottom) reaches 3 9/16 inches (9 cm) in diameter. This end needs to fit into the bottom shaker vessel and rest approximately 1 inch (2.5 cm) below its edge. Check to make sure the flared end of the lid sits at this position. If it rests deeper in the bottom shaker vessel, flare out the base of the lid more. If the lid rests at a more shallow point, stop hammering now.

11 Starting at about 2½ inches (6.4 cm) down from the top of the lid is where the form begins to flare out to a diameter of 3 9/16 (9 cm) inches. Your next goal is to get the area between the 2½-inch (6.4 cm) mark and the wide opening of the lid to flare out even more, creating the wonderful voluminous form that makes the lid look like a traditional shaker. Anneal the lid, and then measure and mark it again with forging guidelines. Refer to the marked guidelines using the narrow lid end as the beginning point: 1 inch (2.5 cm) is 1 inch (2.5 cm) from the top, or the narrow opening of the shaker lid; 2 inches (5 cm) is 2 inches (5 cm) from the top, or narrow opening;

STERLING WORDS

YOU ARE ALWAYS MAKING MORE
WORK FOR YOURSELF IF YOU
DON'T RE-ANNEAL.

and so forth. Forge the metal to stretch it farther between the 3-inch (7.6 cm) and the 3½-inch (8.9 cm) marks than anywhere else on the lid (see photo 6). Expand this area so the direction of the flare and the overall shape of the lid inversely matches the bottom shaker vessel. Designate the 3½-inch (8.9 cm) line as the greatest expansion point of the entire piece, and don't forge or stretch the rest of the areas as much. I recommend forging from the 5½-inch (14 cm) to the 2½-inch (6.4 cm) mark, and then planishing and annealing the lid. Next, forge from the 5-inch (12.7 cm) to the 2½-inch (6.4 cm) mark, then planish and anneal; then from the 4½-inch

(11.4 cm) to the 2½-inch mark (6.4 cm), planish and anneal; and so forth, moving down the lid in ½-inch (1.3 cm) increments. Make your final hammering turn between the 3-inch (7.6 cm) mark and the 3½-inch (8.9 cm) mark. This way, the 3½-inch (8.9 cm) line, the point of greatest expansion, receives the most hammering. This is an interesting form to shape, but it does take time. Make sure to planish between forgings. And then planish. And planish. And planish. Always remember to anneal, or you'll destroy the metal. And don't forget to take breaks—the consequences of hammering too hard for too long can be much worse than destroying the metal!

12 Make final adjustments to the shape of the shaker vessel and its lid. Put the two parts together to see if they fit. Make sure the lid rests snugly within the base and 1 inch (2.5 cm) below its edge so the shaker forms the proper seal for optimum use. If the parts don't fit well, you may need to forge and planish more.

Soldering the Top to the Shaker Lid

13 Check the top opening of the shaker lid against a circle template to make sure it's true. Reshape as needed. File or sand the top edges of the lid so they're flat, flush, and ready for soldering. File the edges of the 2½-inch-diameter (6.4 cm) sterling silver disk, and then hard-solder it to the top of the lid. (Once again, you're soldering together a large and a small piece, so carefully control the heat of the torch.) This connection could take several tries, but don't worry. Take your time and get it right. Let the fully soldered shaker lid cool. Pickle, rinse, and dry it.

14 Use the jeweler's saw to cut off any excess silver from around the top of the lid. File off all excess solder. Pour water in both parts of the shaker, and put them down on a dry surface to make sure there aren't any leaks. If there is a leak, fix it now. If the shaker is watertight, empty the water, fit the pieces together, and step back for a look.

15 Tape a sheet of sandpaper or emery cloth to a level and sturdy surface. Rest the opening of one part of the shaker on the paper. Rub it back and forth over the paper until its edge is flat and even. Repeat this process on the second shaker part. Lightly file the edges of both shaker elements to remove any burrs. Fit the shaker together, and take a break. (The next part, cleaning, isn't anybody's favorite, so you may as well be rested and rejuvenated before you begin!)

Polishing the Shaker

16 Attach one large stitched muslin wheel to the polishing lathe. (If you aren't overly concerned with preserving the planishing marks, you can attach an abrasive wheel to the lathe's second arbor.) Use tripoli compound to remove all firescale from both parts of the shaker. Also remove all file marks and scratches. This stage of polishing will take time. It is a very long process. Make sure the lathe stands at a comfortable height, and that you take frequent breaks. Wash the shaker in hot soapy water. Rinse and dry it. Clean your polishing station and store the tripoli supplies.

17 Attach a stitched muslin wheel and a balloon muslin wheel to the arbors of the polishing lathe. Polish the shaker vessel and its lid with white diamond compound. Start polishing with the stitched muslin wheel, and finish polishing with the balloon wheel. (The stitched wheel cuts the silver surface slightly more than the balloon wheel, and the balloon wheel leaves a slightly higher shine.) Wash the shaker parts in hot soapy water and dry them. Check very closely to make certain there is no firescale left on the cocktail shaker. If there are tiny bits of firescale, you can remove them with the white diamond compound. If there are large firescale areas, mark them with a felt-tip pen, revert to the tripoli-polishing setup, repeat step 16 to polish and clean the shaker again, and then return to the white diamond compound. With careful polishing and inspection, you won't have to go back and forth too often. Clean your polishing station and store the white diamond supplies.

18 Attach one rouge infused wheel (stitched or balloon, whichever you're more comfortable with) and one clean balloon wheel to the polishing lathe arbors. Burnish the cocktail shaker with rouge compound. Buff both pieces with the infused wheel, and dust off the excess compound with the clean balloon wheel. Wash the shaker in hot soapy water, and pat it dry. Clean your polishing station and store the rouge supplies.

Creamer & Sugar Bowl

Here's a challenging project that puts all of your silversmithing skills to work. Getting to use these magnificent pieces every day, however, is worth the effort.

WHAT YOU NEED

Materials

2 sterling silver disks, 18 gauge, 6 inches (15.2 cm) in diameter

Sterling silver sheet, 18 gauge, 2¾ inches (7 cm) square

Hard, medium, and easy solder

Sterling silver sheet, 18 gauge, 8 x ¼ inch (20.3 x .6 cm)

Sterling silver disk, 18 gauge, 2¼ inches (5.7 cm) in diameter

Sterling silver sheet, 18 gauge, 5¹³⁄₁₆ x ¼ inch (14.8 x .6 cm)

Sterling silver sheet, 18 gauge, ¼ x ⅞ inch (.6 x 2.2 cm)

Small wood dowel, less than ¼ inch (6 mm) in diameter

Epoxy

Hammers

Sinking hammer

Forging hammer

Planishing hammer

Rawhide or wooden mallet

Chasing hammer

WHILE YOU CREATE THIS PROJECT,
THE METAL IS GOING TO
WORK-HARDEN VERY QUICKLY
AND REQUIRE FREQUENT ANNEAL-
ING. WHILE IT'S PICKLING, WHY
NOT TAKE A BREAK?

Other Tools

Files

Needle files

Sandpaper or emery cloth

Compass

Dapping block

T-stake

Jeweler's saw and saw blades

Mushroom stake

Vise

Center punch

Swage block or anvil

Drill bit, 1 mm

Calipers

Sheers (optional)

Sandbag (optional)

Steel wool

Wood dowel, $5/16$ inch (3 mm)
in diameter

Acetone

Burnisher

Kits

Soldering kit, page 47

Polishing kit, page 47

Techniques

Filing, page 15

Sinking, page 29

Forging, page 23

Raising, page 29

Sawing, page 12

Planishing, page 28

Piercing, page 13

Soldering, page 35

Polishing, page 44

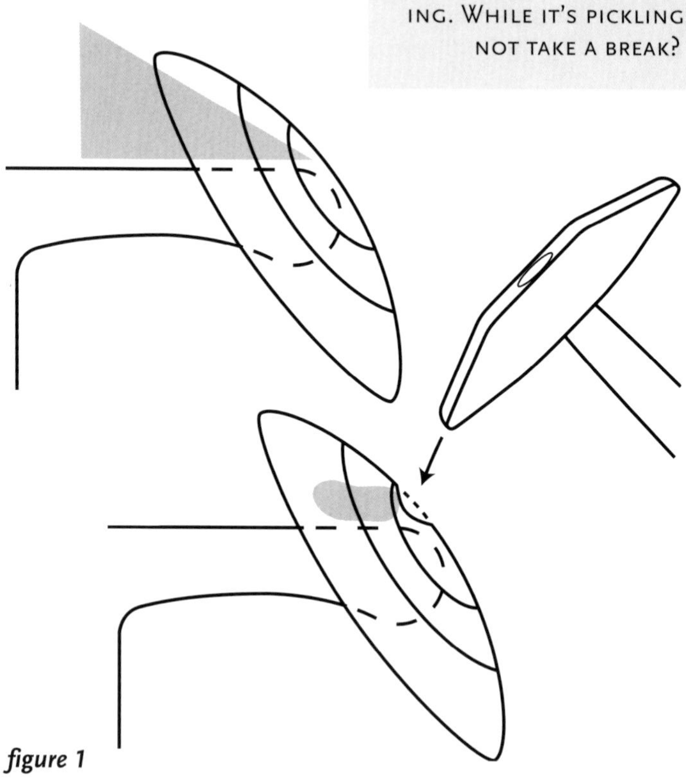

figure 1

WHAT YOU DO

Sinking the Silver & First-Turn Raising

1 File the edges of the 6-inch (15.2 cm) sterling silver disks. Anneal the disks. Use a compass and a felt-tip pen to mark concentric circles on both sides of the disks, each approximately $1/2$ to $3/4$ inch (1.3 to 1.9 cm) apart.

2 Place one marked silver disk on top of a dapping block and use a sinking hammer to sink the disk approximately 1 inch (2.5 cm). Repeat this process to sink the second disk. Re-anneal, pickle, and then mark concentric circles on the disks again, but this time only mark the outside of the disks.

3 Set up the T-stake and have the forging hammer handy. Rest one disk on the T-stake with its innermost marked circle resting on the stake's edge. Angle the disk about 25 to 45 degrees above the stake as shown in figure 1. There must be hammering space between the disk and the stake in order to hit and move the metal (again, see figure 1).

4 Use the forging hammer to hit the disk above and over the edge of the stake. Hammer the silver just above the innermost circle line. Make sure to keep your non-hammering hand out of the way.

(You may want to use it to hold the disk just under the stake. I often wear a glove on my grip hand simply to prevent the shock of the hammer blows from rubbing the disk uncomfortably against my skin.) Continue forging the metal all the way around the innermost circle of the disk.

5 Slightly shift the disk on the stake so it rests on the edge of the forged area. Continue hammering, forging the metal in circles, up and into itself. The further from the center of the disk you hammer, the more difficult this process becomes. (Essentially, you're raising the silver. This is the time you really get to use your hammer to the fullest. Don't be gentle. Raising silver requires brute force. You're wailing on the metal, pushing it into itself, and it will "fight" back. Planishing metal is finesse hammering and positively genteel in comparison. Don't worry about scarring the metal. Don't worry about it being pretty. Wear comfortable clothes and make sure to wear safety glasses. Be prepared to get dirty and to work hard. Raising is difficult, but it's so satisfying when you have a complete piece.) The metal will work-harden very quickly during this project and will need constant annealing. After you've completed the first full raising turn, anneal the silver. Do not forge the entire surface more than once without annealing. If you keep forging and raising without annealing, the metal will no longer move, and its structure can become terminally damaged.

Troubleshooting

During raising, the disk will look nothing like a bowl. It may take on weird shapes and flare out, but don't worry. This is normal. Here are two common incorrectly raised forms and their possible causes.

• The disk may look more like a heavily beaten-up funnel, as shown in photo 1. This shape illustrates a piece that was correctly raised at the beginning, but not enough force was used when the outer turns were hammered. The disk also may have become too hardened or may have been held over the stake at an incorrect angle as hammering progressed, resulting in insufficient space for the metal to correctly move.

• The disk may seem not to have changed dimensions at all and now just looks more beaten up (see photo 2). The metal didn't move much, either because it wasn't positioned correctly (the disk wasn't held at an angle high enough off the stake) or because it wasn't being hit in the correct location (the metal was hit directly on the stake instead of on the area just off it).

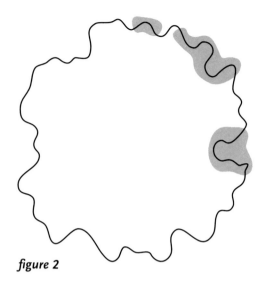

figure 2

Raising the Second Full Turn

6 Redraw the concentric circles on the outside of the disk and prepare to hammer again on the stake. Starting from the innermost circle and keeping the disk at the appropriate angle, use the forging hammer to hit the disk HARD. Turn and hammer the metal all the way around the disk. (The bowl will get wrinkles and folds and look funky. Don't fight it. Those wrinkles are your friends, at least for a short time. Those wrinkles are a good thing, as long as they never turn in on themselves. You can use these qualities to your advantage. It's the folds you have to be careful about.) Move up the disk slightly and hit more. Let the wrinkles form, but just keep them under control. Figure 2 shows places where you should hammer with caution. You don't want the metal to fold. It can't take the stress of forging. It's also exceptionally difficult to get rid of folds. They threaten the integrity of the metal and can cause tears.

7 In figure 3, the highlighted area under the lines represents the wrinkles and folds that are appearing on the silver. This is where you can start to hit the wrinkles into themselves. If you're still raising the area below that line, keep on working, but if the disk is elevated to the desired width, then it's time to start working the wrinkles into themselves. This process also involves brute force. Use the forging hammer to hit the high points of the metal at the lower part of the bend, moving the top of the wrinkle into itself (see the upper highlighted area in figure 3). Be careful not to cause the metal to move over itself, creating a crease or fold that will crack. (You're working hard to thicken the material, but folding it won't accomplish this goal.) Raising is a slow silversmithing technique that starts in the center and progresses outward—the opposite of

sinking. Continue to hammer around the entire bowl until it's work-hardened. Remember to always work in circles from the center, climbing up and out on the disk. Work from the area that needs the least motion to the area that needs the most. Raise both 6-inch (15.2 cm) disks for quite some time, until they both come up at an angle of about 67 degrees (see photo 3). At this point, most of the waves and wrinkles in the silver should be removed, and you should have two small vessels.

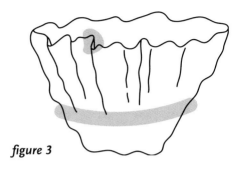

figure 3

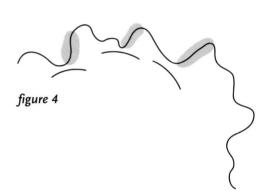

figure 4

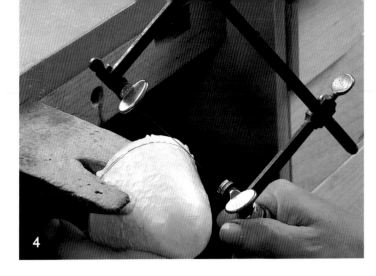

4

5

Necking the Sugar Bowl & the Creamer

8 Measure the height of each raised silver vessel. If it's more than 3½ inches (8.9 cm) tall, use the jeweler's saw to cut off the excess silver above the 3½-inch (8.9 cm) point.

Hint: To saw a large shape like this vessel, rest it on an existing bench pin or create a bench pin on which it can rest. Make small cuts that move along the marked line. Gently saw all the way around the vessel, and then go around again and again until you saw through it (see photo 4). This process takes time, but it's the best way to cleanly and uniformly remove the extra lip.

9 Necking one of the little vessels to use as the sugar bowl takes even more brute force. Select one vessel to use as the bowl and mark it 2 inches (5 cm) up from its base. Rest the bowl on the T stake at the marked line. Allow for a deep angle so that when you hit the bowl, you'll really get the metal moving. Use the forging hammer to hit the silver on the line all the way around the bowl (see photo 5). Don't worry about causing any wrinkles in the metal. In fact, you'll be exaggerating them as shown in figure 4.

6

THE PROJECTS

10 Place the sugar bowl on the T-stake. Using the forging hammer crosswise so it matches the direction the metal is moving, hit more in any area that curved inward to exaggerate the wrinkles (see photo 6). Using raising techniques, hit into the wrinkles to thicken the metal. Once you finish the first round of necking, the sides of the bowl may stand straight up. If they do, repeat the process to bring in the bowl's upper edges. This technique takes lots of time, lots of practice, and lots of patience to master (and even more to enjoy! If you get frustrated, remember to take it out on the wrinkles and bends of the metal, and not your friends and neighbors.).

Hint: Don't press too hard on the stake. Every hammer blow you make carries force that has to go somewhere. If you're pressing too hard on the stake, you run the risk of stretching the sides of the bowl out rather than thickening its neck in. With too much pressure and stretching, you can hammer right through the sides of the bowl. Not fun. That's one reason you're only raising a gentle neck for this vessel.

11 Raising is a variable technique. Each person does it a little differently with different results. You'll probably end up with excess metal from stretching the bowl up. Too much metal makes necking more difficult, so if you trim the silver before continuing to neck, you'll have less metal to move. Use a jeweler's saw or a file to remove extra silver. Neck the sugar bowl until its opening is 2 to 2¼ inches (5 to 5.7 cm) in diameter.

12 Repeat steps 8 to 11 to neck the second sterling silver vessel for the creamer. Only neck the creamer to 2¾ inches (7 cm) in diameter. Anneal the sugar bowl and the creamer. Let the vessels cool, and then pickle, rinse, and dry them. Clean up your hammering station and put away the forging hammer.

Planishing the Creamer & the Sugar Bowl

13 Set up the mushroom stake and prepare to planish. Mark concentric circles on the outside of both vessels, each ½ inch (1.3 cm) apart. These guidelines help you hammer in an orderly sequence so you'll create nicely formed shapes. Rest one vessel on the mushroom stake. Use the planishing hammer to clean up as many forging marks as possible. Start from the innermost circle and slowly planish to the top of the vessel. Follow the guidelines and turn the vessel as needed. If the bottom of the vessel was flat, planishing will curve it, and that's fine. If the bottom was curved from earlier sinking, that's fine, too. You're planishing to give the pieces a more uniform surface texture and a more uniform form. Repeat this step to planish the second vessel as thoroughly as possible.

14 Switch to the T-stake and continue planishing. This stake change will help you reach the necked areas of the vessels. Hammering with control matters a great deal here, so if you're tired, take a break. You want to work with consistency, finesse, and sharp focus to bring accurate and attractive curves to the silver forms. The planishing smooths the vessel surfaces and edges, giving them a more consistent overall shape. You always want to hammer in the same direction, so start planishing at the widest part of the necked area and move up in concentric circles toward the vessel opening. Hammer hardest where you need to stretch the metal the most and lightest where you need to stretch the metal less. As you get close to the correct vessel shape, make more uniform hammer blows in order to ensure a pleasant surface without any forging marks. You won't remove all the forging marks on the first pass, so anneal the piece and planish again. You'll have to planish both the creamer and the sugar bowl more than once to achieve their correct form and dimensions.

15 To ensure that the creamer and the sugar bowl openings are true round, draw a precise template on a piece of paper and check the vessel openings against it. To ensure that the vessel shapes are as close to spherical as possible, cut out a cardboard template that represents the precise wall curve of the vessels. Rest the cardboard template against the side of one vessel and rotate it, watching for any areas that don't cleanly fit within and against the template. Mark any trouble spots with a felt-tip pen and correct them as much as possible. It will be much easier to flare out any recessed areas than to force in the metal. Repeat this process on the second vessel.

THE PROJECTS

7

Making the Creamer Spout

16 Put the forging hammer in the vise, angled side facing up, to use as a stake. Rest the creamer neck on the hammer/stake and hit it with a rawhide or wooden mallet to shape its spout as shown in photo 7. Stretching one area of the opening to make the spout can draw in other neck areas. Use this to your advantage. You'll have to planish the creamer again once the spout is formed, but you won't have to neck the creamer as much as the sugar bowl to achieve the final shape. By simply making the spout the metal will be sufficiently moved.

17 Replanish the creamer in circles around the form as much as possible without disturbing the spout. Skip that area as you hammer. If you didn't planish the spout when you pulled it out on the stake, you may want to do so now. Hardening the spout will help it keep its shape. Figure 5 illustrates the different surfaces, areas, and directions for planishing the creamer. The bottom half, which is not marked, should be hammered in normal planishing circles. The directions on the spout flow with the direction you've already moved the metal. Using the forging hammer as a stake will continue to be useful when planishing the creamer. The arrow at the edge of and just outside the spout represents the line of planishing required along the edge of the spout.

18 Use the templates created in step 15 to see if the creamer shape is true. Rest its opening against the drawn circle to see if it matches. (The spout will extend beyond the edge of the template.) Rotate the cardboard template around the creamer, excluding its spout, and check to see that it's also true to form. When the templates match the openings and bodies of both the creamer and the sugar bowl and when both forms are fully planished and free of all marks made by hammers (other than the planishing hammer), you're really making progress!

19 One at a time, rest the openings of both the creamer and the sugar bowl on top of sandpaper or emery cloth. Rub each piece back and forth across the paper to smooth its edges. Both vessels need to have completely flat and true edges all the way around their openings.

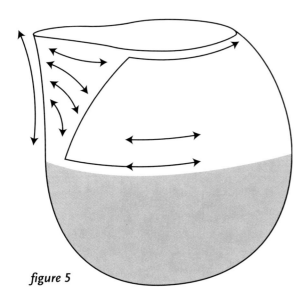

figure 5

Soldering the Top Ring to the Sugar Bowl

20 Use the compass to precisely mark a 2¾-inch (6.9 cm) disk on the 2¾-inch (6.9 cm) square sterling silver sheet. Using the jeweler's saw, cut out the disk. The size of each sugar bowl lip will vary slightly from person to person. Measure and mark a circle on the silver disk that reflects your bowl's lip, and then find and mark its center. Use the compass to make a centered interior circle with a 1⅛-inch diameter within the unique circle shape. Dimple, drill, and then saw out the interior circle. Now you have an 0-shaped silver piece with a marked line that corresponds to the sugar bowl opening.

21 Flux the edge of the sugar bowl opening and the 0-shaped silver piece, and hard-solder them together. (I recommend using hard solder because this connection isn't the only seam on this piece and because hard solder is closest in color to sterling silver, leaving the least noticeable seam.) If you find the bowl edge and the 0-shaped piece won't fully solder the first time, feel free to use any of the tricks you've learned. For example, you could tack-solder the seam; cool, pickle, rinse, and dry it; and then press the metal, either with your hands or a mallet, to get it to rest against the bowl edge, and try again to solder the seam. Once the 0-shaped piece is completely attached to the sugar bowl, pickle, rinse, and dry it.

22 Use the jeweler's saw to cut off all excess silver from around the edge of the sugar bowl. In order to cleanly cut the metal and reduce subsequent filing, hold the saw frame at an unusual angle and keep it that way. Once you've trimmed as much excess silver as possible with the saw, use the files to remove any remaining metal and solder. Use the calipers to see if the sugar bowl lip's interior edge is equidistant from its exterior edge at all points around the vessel. If the measurements are inconsistent, use the most narrow dimension and mark the bowl all the way around the lip at that point. File away all silver that extends past the marked line.

Making the Notch for the Sugar Spoon (Optional)

23 Make two marks on the lip of the sugar bowl, each perpendicular to both the interior and exterior edge of the lip. Draw the marks ⅛ inch (3 mm) apart and approximately 3⁄16 inch (5 mm) in from the interior edge. Use a file to carve away the metal within the marks, or, if you're comfortable using abrasive wheels on a flexible shaft, you can use them to create this notch. (By using old-fashioned hand tools, you'll eliminate the risk of making a major mistake and wasting a great deal of silver.) Use the needle files to smooth the edges of the sugar bowl. Remove all burrs or surface disturbances.

8

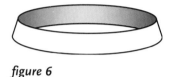

figure 6

THE PROJECTS

Making the Base Rings

24 Use the jeweler's saw or shears to cut the 8 x ¼-inch (20.3 x .6 cm) sterling silver strip in half. Both bases will be the same size and shape. Bend each of the cut strips so their ends meet, and hard-solder them into rings. Quench, pickle, rinse, and dry the rings. File off any excess solder. Move to your hammer station. Rest one soldered ring on the T-stake and planish it into a circle. (Planishing makes the rings more uniform and creates a surface texture that complements the rest of the piece.) Planish the second ring. Hammering harder on one edge of the ring will cause it to flare out as shown in photo 8 and figure 6. This decorative detail can make the base more attractive, and it will add to the stability of the finished form. File the edges of both rings. Both sides must be smooth, and the whole ring needs to remain a uniform width. Pay careful attention. You need to make even and level platforms for the creamer and sugar bowl.

Attaching the Base Rings

25 Place the creamer and the sugar bowl upside down on your work bench. Use a measuring tool or a grounded caliper and a felt-tip pen to find the exact center of the base of each vessel. For the creamer and sugar bowl to look like a set, they must have precisely centered bases that sit well and look uniform. Mark a ring on each vessel that matches the silver base ring and is equidistant from the center mark. If you flared the base rings out as shown in photo 8, rest their smaller edges on the vessels to achieve the most support.

26 Cut pallions of lower temperature solder. (I recommend pallion soldering because you'll be working on a form that will be difficult to clean. The less solder you spread, the less cleaning you'll have to do.) Pay close attention to what you're doing at all times. You're soldering a very large piece of silver (the vessel) to a small piece (the base ring) that was previously soldered. Take your time and concentrate

the heat on the larger silver areas. The base ring will heat up with the larger piece. Once the solder is ready to flow and flowing in the correct manner, the large and small silver pieces will start becoming one, and you'll still want to concentrate the heat on the larger areas.

Note: You'll develop and understand this technique to the point where you no longer need to think about it. It becomes second nature, like breathing. It's something you have to do, even if it eventually requires little thought. This is true of much of the mundane silversmithing work. Even though it may seem repetitive, redundant, and brainless, like breathing, you can't get away without doing it.)

Fully solder one base ring to the creamer and one base ring to the sugar bowl. (You're really making progress now!) Let them cool. Pickle, rinse, and dry the vessels.

9

27 Set down the creamer and the sugar bowl, step back, and take a look. Do they look even? Uniform? Like a set? Is anything noticeably wrong at this point? If there are problems, correct them now. If you soldered a base on and it isn't centered, you may want to remove and then reattach it. If you take this step, make sure to clean off all solder from the vessel prior to resoldering the base. (Cleaning off old solder after you reattach the base is much more difficult and time-consuming.)

Making the Sugar Bowl Lid

28 The sugar bowl opening measures approximately 1⅞ inches (4.8 cm) in diameter. Let's round that figure up to 2 inches (5 cm). The curve of the lid needs to be larger than this measurement, so use the 2¼-inch (5.7 cm) sterling silver disk to construct this element. Place the disk on a dapping block or sandbag and use the sinking hammer to gently dome the lid. Don't sink too much of a curve. The lid should be in aesthetic agreement with the overall form of the sugar bowl. Draw concentric circle hammering guidelines on the sunken lid. (Even a piece as small as a lid can become out of true. If the silver is properly marked, it's easier to catch and correct mistakes early.) Place the domed and marked lid on a mushroom stake and planish it. You can probably planish the whole form fairly easily without needing to anneal it, but use your judgment. If the metal is too hard or a bit out of true and you think it will work better softened, then anneal it.

29 Draw a precise 2¼-inch (5.7 cm) circle on a piece of paper. Rest the lid on the circle template to make sure its shape is accurate. Step back from the lid and check to see that its dome is nice and uniform. Once you're satisfied and have planished the lid's surface to match the sugar bowl, file its edges smooth. Since the lid rests against the sugar bowl, its edges must be clean and uniform. With its edges facing down, place the lid on sandpaper or emery paper attached to a flat surface. Rub the lid back and forth across the paper until all edges are completely level. Recheck the lid against the circle template to make sure it's still true. Use the needle files to clean up any burrs or sharp edges on the lip.

Making the Sugar Bowl Lid's Inner Lip

30 Bend the ends of the 5 ¹³⁄₁₆ x ¼-inch (14.7 x .6 cm) sterling silver strip until they meet and form a ring. (I made this measurement a bit on the small side because it's easier to stretch metal than to shrink it.) Hard-solder together the ring. Pickle, rinse, and dry it. Use the files to remove any excess solder. Working at your hammer station, use the planish-

ing hammer to hit the ring on the T-stake until it's round. (Don't hit too hard. You don't want to stretch the metal until you're certain it's necessary.) Check the diameter of the ring against the diameter of the sugar bowl opening. If the ring is too small, planish it more to stretch it to the appropriate diameter. The ring should be the right size to help gently steer the lid to the correct location on the bowl and hold it there. If the fit is too tight, it will be difficult for you to put the lid on and off. Once the ring is the appropriate diameter, rub it on the sandpaper to smooth its edges. Use the needle files to remove any burrs. Recheck the ring against a circle template to ensure it has remained true round.

31 Use the calipers and a felt-tip pen to mark a circle inside the lid indicating where the ring needs to be soldered. This helps ensure the ring is centered so the lid sits in the correct location. Flux the lid and the ring, and solder them together with pallions of medium solder as shown in photo 9. Remember the rules for heating and attaching large and small pieces. Let the lid cool. Pickle, rinse, and dry it.

10

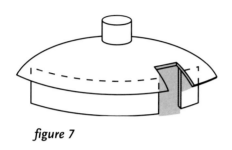
figure 7

Making the Button for the Lid

32 Bend the ends of the 1/4 x 7/8-inch (.6 x 2.2 cm) sterling silver strip until they meet and form a ring. Hard-solder together the ring. Pickle and rinse it. File all excess solder off the interior and the exterior of the ring. Bring the form to true round. (You can use a wood dowel that fits within the ring and a mallet to help you.) Smooth any rough ring edges with files or sandpaper. Easy-solder the ring to the center of the top of the lid. (If you put pallions inside the ring, there will be less solder mess to clean.) Let the lid cool. Pickle, rinse, and dry it. Take a breather!

Rough-Cleaning the Creamer & the Sugar Bowl

33 Thoroughly examine the creamer and the sugar bowl. Look for excess solder, burrs, pits, or marks, and remove all of them. Use the files, needle files, emery cloth, sandpaper, sanding sticks, or whatever you have at hand to improve the areas that need rough cleaning.

Note: This slow and deliberate process may make you want to get up and scream. I don't recommend the second part, but I do recommend you get up and stretch. Paying such close attention to detail, combined with the meticulous nature of filing can really strain your body, eyes, mind, neck, shoulders, arms, wrists, hands, and fingers. I urge you to get up and move about. Stretch. Wave. Move your body. When a piece requires substantial cleaning time, you need to spend equal time moving your body in opposing directions. Making your blood flow will also help you stay alert.

Notching the Sugar Bowl Lid
(Optional)

34 Make two marks on the edge of the sugar bowl lid, each perpendicular to the edge of the interior lip. Place the marks 1/8 inch (3 mm) apart and 3/16 inch (5 mm) in from the edge. Use the jeweler's saw to cut away a matching notch in the lid. As shown in figure 7, cut in far enough to remove some of the inner lip of the lid. Use the needle files to smooth all cut edges.

Polishing & Finishing the Creamer & the Sugar Bowl

35 Attach a stitched muslin wheel to the polishing lathe and prepare it with tripoli compound. (If you want to remove the firescale more quickly and you're not overly attached to the planishing hammer marks, you can start with a more abrasive wheel.) I recommend polishing the lips and the edges of the creamer, the sugar bowl, and its lid first. Don't polish against the edge, and don't get the edges caught. Simply clean up and shine these surfaces, making sure they're equally worked.

36 Polish the bodies of the creamer, the sugar bowl, and its lid with the tripoli compound. The curved and spherical shapes of these pieces make cleaning and polishing them fairly simple. There aren't many difficult angles and cuts to navigate. When you reach the base ring of the creamer and the sugar bowl, be gentle. As shown in photo 10, make sure to get into the corners where the base rings and the vessels meet. (If you don't remove all the firescale, the areas you miss will become darker and the stains more evident over time. It is noticeable, even to a novice, and it isn't pretty.)

11

Rotate the pieces as you polish. (To clean the outer ledge of the underside of the lid, you may want to use a smaller wheel or even the flexible shaft. If you don't wish to clean inside and underneath the lid or the insides of the creamer and sugar bowl, you certainly don't have to.) Once you've completely polished each piece with tripoli compound, take a break, and then check again for firescale. If you spot any, remove it now before proceeding to the white diamond compound. Rinse the silver pieces in hot soapy water. Clean your polishing station and store the tripoli supplies.

37 Use the steel wool to scrub inside the creamer, the sugar bowl, and its lid (see photo 11). These areas are too deep to polish well on the lathe. Rather than using the wheel, you're going to use the traditional method of cleaning the interior of a deep vessel. You're going to give the pieces a "brushed" or "scratched" finish. With all of the annealing and pickling the creamer and the sugar bowl have been subject to, their interior surfaces should look rather bright white. That's good. That color indicates a fine silver surface, which is desirable. It won't tarnish, and it won't impart flavor to the cream. Lightly rub the vessel interiors

with the steel wool. You can do this dry or put on some cleaning gloves and do it with soap and water. I recommend the latter because it facilitates a more uniform surface and helps prevent the steel wool particles from becoming airborne. Be very careful not to rub the steel wool on the sides of the silver. You'll have to polish out any scratches you make. Rinse each piece in hot soapy water several times. Rinse again, and again, and again. You don't want bits of steel wool contaminating the next polishing wheels. Dry the creamer, the sugar bowl, and its lid.

38 Place one stitched wheel and one balloon wheel on the arbors of the lathe. Polish each piece with the white diamond compound. Remember to take extra special care around edges and soldered connections. Check the creamer, the sugar bowl, and its lid for firescale. Circle any areas you may find, prepare your polishing area and wheels for tripoli, and repeat step 36 and step 38. If you did a great job with the tripoli compound on the first pass, you won't have any firescale. Wash the creamer, the sugar bowl, and its lid in hot soapy water. Rinse and dry the pieces. Clean your polishing station and store the white diamond supplies.

39 Use the jeweler's saw to cut a 1/4-inch (6 mm) piece of the 5/16-inch-diameter (3 mm) wood dowel to place inside the sugar lid button. If the dowel piece is too large, carefully and slowly file it down until it fits. Taper your filing so that the end that goes first into the button is more narrow than the exposed end. Leave this end textured and marred. Before you install the dowel, place a small amount of epoxy inside the button. Tap the wood dowel into place. If any epoxy runs out, immediately wipe it up with acetone so it won't stick to the surface of the sugar bowl lid. Let the epoxy dry completely. Cut off any excess wood, and then sand it flush with the silver. Use the burnisher to rub off any filing or sanding marks on the edge of the button.

40 Attach one balloon wheel and one clean dusting wheel to the polishing lathe. Polish the creamer, the sugar bowl, and its lid with the balloon wheel and the rouge compound. Be careful when polishing the button on the lid because the rouge compound can stain the wood dowel. Use the clean dusting wheel to dust off any streaked areas. Clean the silver pieces in hot soapy water and pat them dry. Be sure to pat-dry the interior of the creamer and the sugar bowl so none of the rouge compound stains these areas. Do a little dance of happiness, take a bow, take a breather, and enjoy your new silver cream and sugar set!

Gallery

▼ **THOMAS P. MUIR**
Double-Walled Bowl, 1983
Sterling silver, nickel
3 x 7 x 7 in. (7.6 x 17.7 x 17.8 cm)
Private collection
Photo by artist

◄ **THOMAS P. MUIR**
*Cycladic Figure
With His Hair in a Roller
(Espresso Server),* 1986
Sterling silver, nickel,
anodized aluminum
11½ x 3 x 4 in.
(29.2 x 6.4 x 10.2 cm)
Collection of the
Art Institute of Chicago
Photo by Bob Viglletti

THOMAS P. MUIR ►
Orchid Vase, 1997
Sterling silver
11½ x 4¾ x 4¾ in.
(29.2 x 12.1 x 12.1 cm)
Photo by Tim Thayer

◄ **THOMAS P. MUIR**
*Cycladic Figure Impregnated
(Espresso Server),* 1987
Sterling silver, oxidized
copper, anodized
aluminum, 18 karat gold
11½ x 3 x 4 in.
(29.2 x 7.6 x 10.2 cm)
Photo by Rob Wheless

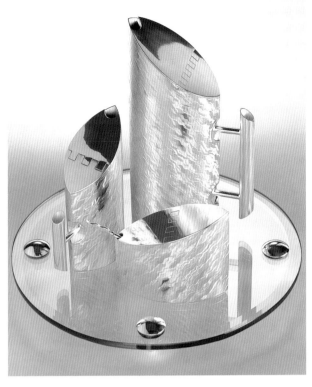

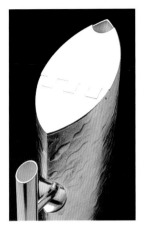

◀ KEVIN O'DWYER
Coffee Service
(detail: creamer hinge)

▲ KEVIN O'DWYER
Coffee Service, 1996
Sterling silver, glass: formed,
fabricated, engraved
Coffee pot: 12 in. (30.5 cm) high
Photo by Robert Walker

KEVIN O'DWYER ▲
Mad-Hatter's Teapot, 1992
Patterned sterling silver: formed,
fabricated, hand forged
11 in. (28 cm) high
Photo by James Fratter

◀ ALEX BERNARD
Tab Tea Set, 2002
Sterling silver, acrylic, nylon:
spinning, fabrication
Teapot: 24 x 15 x 12 cm; sugar bowl:
6 x 10 x 10 cm; milk jug: 10 x 7 x 6 cm
Photo by Clarissa Bruce

◄ **MICHAEL AND MAUREEN BANNER**
Kiddush Cups and Candleholders, 1993
Sterling silver: handwrought, spun, raised,
planished, hollow formed
Candleholders: 10 in. (25.4 cm) high;
cups: 8 in. (20.3 cm) high
Photo by Paul Rocheleau

MICHAEL AND MAUREEN BANNER ►
Pagoda, 2000
Sterling silver teapot, rosewood handle spacers:
handwrought, hollow formed, raised
16 in. (40.6 cm) high
Photo by Paul Rocheleau

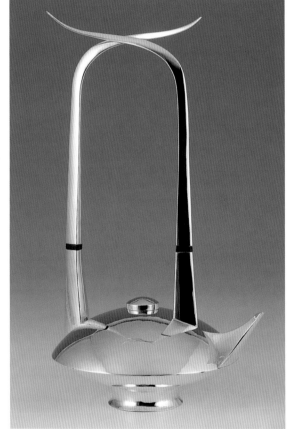

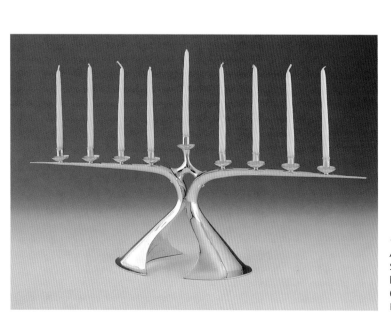

◄ **MICHAEL AND MAUREEN BANNER**
Arms, 1995
Sterling silver Hanukkah menorah:
handwrought, hollow formed
6 in. (15.2 cm) high
Photo by Paul Rocheleau

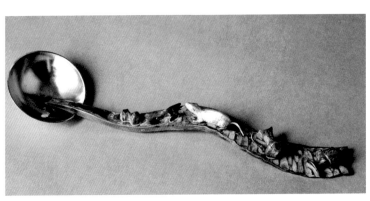

◄ VALENTIN YOTKOV
Bowl, 1997
Copper: raised, chased, patinated
4¾ x 7½ in. (12 x 19 cm)
Photo by Plamen Petkov

▲ ROBERT COOGAN
Like a Rat Through a Maze, 2002
Copper, sterling silver: forged
1 x 9 x 2 in. (2.5 x 22.8 x 5 cm)
Photo by TTU Photo Services

▲ MARTHA JO BENSON
Ginkgo Goblet, 1997
Sterling silver: raised, constructed
5½ x 4 x 4 in. (14 x 10.2 x 10.2 cm)
Photo by Bob Elbert

GALLERY

◄ SARAH PERKINS
Contained Folded Vessel, 1998
Silver, enamel
8 x 4½ x 4½ in. (20.3 x 11.4 x 11.4 cm)
Photo by Tim Barnwell

YOSHIKO YAMAMOTO ▼
A Pair of Goblets, 2000
Sterling silver: raised, fabricated
3¾ x 2¾ x 2½ in. (9.5 x 6.9 x 6.4 cm)
Photo by Dean Powell

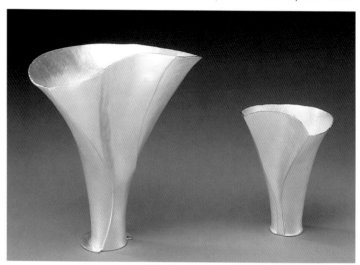

▲ PEGEEN G. MILLER-KERN
Greenhouse Reliquary, 2002
Sterling silver, 24 karat gold
8 x 7 x 7 in. (20.3 x 17.8 x 17.8 cm)
Photo by Tim Thayer

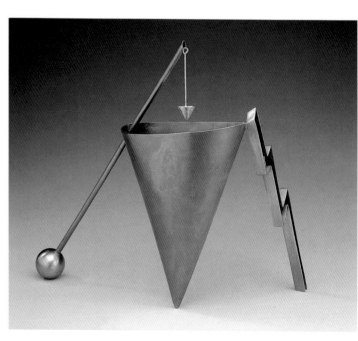

▲ YOSHIKO YAMAMOTO
Equilibrium #2, 1999
Sterling silver, copper: fabricated
7 x 3¾ x 2½ in. (17.8 x 9.5 x 6.4 cm)
Photo by Dean Powell

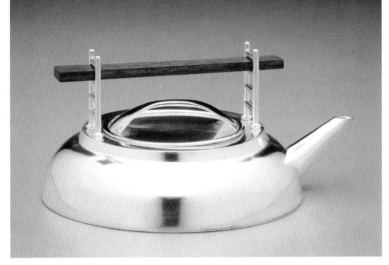

Bridge, 1999
Sterling silver, wood: fabricated, spun
6¼ x 5¼ x 2⅝ in. (15.9 x 13.3 x 6.7 cm)
Photo by Robert H. Hensley

SADIE SHU PING WANG ▶
Four Seasons, 2001
18 karat gold, sterling silver,
copper, resin, cherry
7 x 16½ x 1¼ in. (17.8 x 41.9 x 3.2 cm)
Photo by John Lucas

▲ DEBRA ADELSON
Toddler Feeding Set, 2003
Sterling silver, acrylic: hand-smithed silver,
hand-carved and hand-dyed acrylic
5½ x 9 x 6 in. (13.9 x 22.8 x 15.2 cm)
Photo by Peter Groesbeck

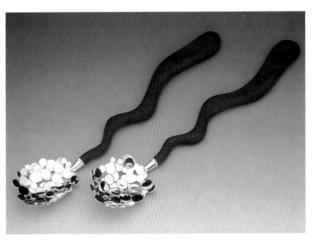

▲ DEBRA ADELSON
Bubbles Salad Server Set, 2003
Sterling silver, acrylic: hand-smithed silver,
hand-carved and hand-dyed acrylic
12 x 3½ x 1 in. (30.5 x 8.9 x 2.5 cm)
Photo by Peter Groesbeck

◄ **JACQUELYN A. CRISSMAN**
Noble Nectar, 2003
Sterling silver, citrine, nylon, patina:
fabrication, chasing, repousse, weaving, patina
9½ x 4½ x 4½ in. (24.1 x 11.4 x 11.4 cm)
Photo by Wired Images (Ericka Crissman)

▼ **JACQUELYN A. CRISSMAN**
Noble Nectar (detail)

JACQUELYN A. CRISSMAN ►
Sweet Disdain Vessel
(a narrative of Aesop's fable,
The Fox and the Grapes), 2003
Sterling silver, fine silver, copper,
patina: fabrication, weaving,
raising, chasing, repousse
4¾ x 3¾ in. (12.1 x 9.5 cm)
Photo by Wired Images
(Erika Crissman)

RICHARD MAWDSLEY ▶
Letter Opener, 1992
Sterling silver, gold plate, garnet,
pattern welded steel (by Daryl Meier)
11 in. (27.9 cm) long
Collection of Mr. and Mrs. Monte Lemann
Photo by Neil Pickett

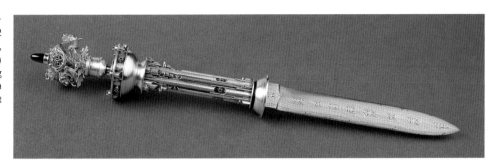

RICHARD MAWDSLEY ▶
Ladle, 1993–94
Sterling silver: fabricated, raised
15 in. (38.1 cm) long
Collection of Kathleen Mawdsley
Photo by Neil Pickett

▲ **RICHARD MAWDSLEY**
Ladle (detail)

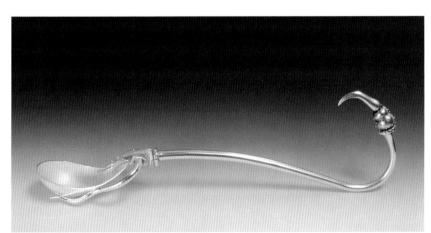

◀ **TIMOTHY LAZURE**
Midnight Snack, 1997
Sterling silver
11 x 3 x 2½ in. (27.9 x 7.6 x 6.4 cm)
Photo by artist

Vase, 1998
Sterling silver: scored, folded, collapsed
10 x 3½ in. (25.4 x 8.9 cm)
Photo by artist

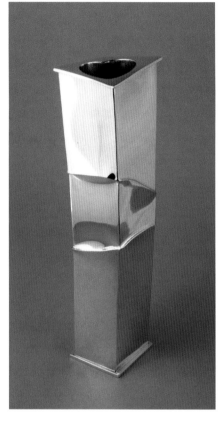

▼ **SIGURD BRONGER**
Salt and Pepper Shakers, 1997
Sterling silver
7.5 x 6 cm
Photo by artist

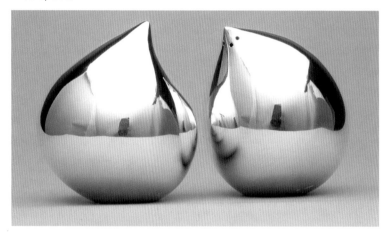

GALLERY

◀ **REBECCA SCHEER**
Futensils: Silverware, 2000–01
Sterling silver, stainless steel, rubies:
forged, constructed
Photo by artist

◄ **MARILYN DA SILVA**
Silver Pear Teapot, 1997
Sterling silver, copper, gesso, colored pencil
3½ x 4 x 2½ in. (8.9 x 10.2 x 6.4 cm)
Photo by Phillip Cohen

MARILYN DA SILVA ►
Tamagosya, 2001
Sterling silver, brass, glass,
wood, gesso, colored pencil, paint
8 x 12 x 5½ in. (20.3 x 30.5 x 13.9 cm)
Photo by M. Lee Fatherree

◄ **JACK P. DA SILVA**
Untitled, 1999
Sterling silver
5 x 12 x 9 in. (12.7 x 30.5 x 22.8 cm)
Photo by M. Lee Fatherree

▲ JULIA WOODMAN
Honeycomb Fish Slicer and Fork, 1991
Sterling silver, vermeil, citrine:
honeycomb tessellated handles
12½ x 3 x 1 in. (31.7 x 7.6 x 2.5 cm)
Photo by artist

▲ JULIA WOODMAN
A Lady's Pearls Ladle and Slicer, 1998
Sterling silver, glass: "Carolina Moon"
and "Jack in the Beanstalk" tessellated handles
15 x 4 x 1 in. (38.1 x 10.2 x 2.5 cm)
Photo by artist

▲ JULIA WOODMAN
The Holy Innocents: Pine Cone Giborium, Chalice, and Paten, 2001
Sterling silver, glass, 18 karat gold, 24 karat gold plate:
pine cone tessellated stem
From left: 5 (diameter) x 4 x 8 in. (12.7 x 10.2 x 20.3 cm);
4½ (diameter) x 3½ x 6½ (11.4 x 8.9 x 16.5 cm);
7⅜ in. (17.7 cm) square
Photo by artist

▼ JULIA WOODMAN
Honeycomb Honey Pot and Dip, 1999
Sterling silver, vermeil: honeycomb
and accordion tessellation
Honey pot: 4 x 3½ in. (10.2 x 8.9 cm);
dip: 5 x 1 in. (12.7 x 2.5 cm)
Photo by artist

◄ **ALEX AUSTIN**
Leaf Aperitif Cups, 2003
Sterling silver
2½ x 2 x 2 in. (6.4 x 5 x 5 cm)
Photo by Ralph Gabriner

▲ **ALEX AUSTIN**
Pierced Tidal Bowl, 1999
Sterling silver
5 x 11 x 8 in. (12.7 x 27.9 x 20.3 cm)
Photo by Ralph Gabriner

▲ **G. PHIL POIRIER**
Grapevine Goblet, 2001
Sterling silver, 18 karat gold, Iolite, amethyst:
hand raised, engraved, chased, repoussé
11 x 5½ x 5½ in. (27.9 x 14 x 14 cm)
Photo by artist

◄ **G. PHIL POIRER**
In the Hip, 2002
Sterling silver, rubies:
constructed, overlaid,
appliquéd, engraved, turned
6 x 3½ x 1 in.
(15.2 x 8.9 x 2.5 cm)
Photo by artist

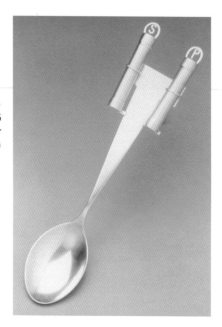

CAROLANNE PATTERSON ▶
Salt and Pepper Spoon, 1996
Sterling silver
8 x 2½ in. (20.3 x 6.4 cm)

▼ PAUL WELLER
Untitled
Sterling silver
From left: 3 x 3 x 3 in. (7.5 x 7.5 x 7.5 cm);
2⅜ x 4¾ x 4 in. (6 x 12 x 10 cm);
2⅜ x 2⅜ x 3⅛ in. (6 x 6 x 8 cm)
Photo by artist

GALLERY

▼ SUSAN R. EWING
Ex Voto to St. Eligius: Loving Cup, 1994
Sterling silver
3 x 10¼ x 4¾ in. (7.6 x 26 x 12 cm)
Photo by Jeffrey Sabo

▲ SUSAN R. EWING
Laughable Loves: Black Heart Vessel, 2000
Sterling silver, patina
6 x 6¼ x 5 in.
(15.2 x 15.8 x 12.7 cm)
Photo by Jeffrey Sabo

◀ **BROOKE MARKS SWANSON**
The Three of Us, 1999
Copper, silver, patina: raised, fabricated
From left: 6½ x 6½ x 13¼ in. (16.5 x 16.5 x 33.6 cm);
9½ x 9½ x 15¼ in. (24.1 x 24.1 x 38.7 cm);
5½ x 5½ x 13 in. (14 x 14 x 33 cm)
Photo by Kevin Montague and Michael Cavanaugh

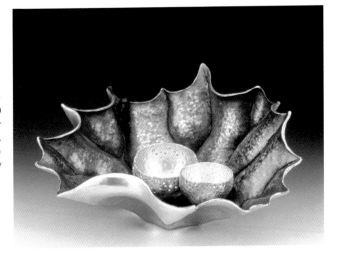

DANIELLE CRISSMAN ▶
Obtaining Balance, 1999
Sterling silver
5¼ x 5 x 2½ in.
(13.3 x 12.7 x 6.4 cm)
Photo by Jerry Anthony

▲ **ANDY COOPERMAN**
Sargasso (fish server), 2002
Sterling silver, 18 karat gold, diamond, pearl:
rolled, forged, fabricated, cast bolster
13 in. (33 cm) long
Photo by Doug Yaple

ANDY COOPERMAN ▶
St. Patrick's Reliquary
(chess piece, black bishop), 2003
Sterling silver, shibuichi, 18 karat gold,
bronze, 7X lens, boa constrictor jaw fragment:
fabricated, forged, riveted
3 in. (7.6 cm) high
Photo by Doug Yaple

BARRY THOMAS ▶
Rabinovitch Fish Slice, 2002
Sterling silver, moonstone
12 in. (30.5 cm)
Photo by artist

◄ BARRY THOMAS
Pentagonal Salt or Pepper Pots, 2001
Sterling silver, gilt
1¾ in. (4.5 cm) high
Photo by artist

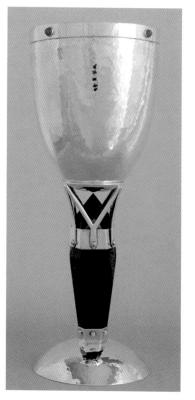

▲ RUTH RHOTEN
Spiral Bowl, 2000
Sterling silver, gold plate
4½ x 10 in. (11.4 x 25.4 cm)
Photo by artist

▲ RUTH RHOTEN
Chalice, 1989
Sterling silver, 18 karat gold, diamond eyes,
rutilated quartz, turquoise
10½ x 4¼ in. (26.7 x 10.8 cm)
Photo by artist

PAMELA MORRIS THOMFORD ▶
For Toddlerboy: Tinkertoy with a Flourish, 1996
Sterling silver, chrysoprase: fabricated
7 x 1½ x 1 in. (17.8 x 3.8 x 2.5 cm)
Photo by Tim Thayer

◀ JULIA WOODMAN
Honeycomb Kiddush Cups, 1991
Sterling silver, vermeil: honeycomb tessellated stems
6 x 2½ in. (15.2 x 6.4 cm)
Photo by artist

▲ YAAKOV GREENVURCEL
Salt and Pepper Shakers, 2001
Sterling silver: constructed, soldered
4 in. (10.2 cm) high
Photo by Baruch Rimon

▲ YAAKOV GREENVURCEL
Honey and Apple Dish for Rosh Hashanah, 2000
Sterling silver: spun, cut, soldered
9 in. (22.9 cm) diameter
Photo by Baruch Rimon

Gallery Artist Profiles

DEBRA ADELSON
Philadelphia, Pennsylvania
www.funkyflatware.com
Adelson creates tableware, gift items, and Judaica in silver and acrylic. She graduated in 1996 from the Tyler School of Art. Her work has appeared in the Smithsonian Craft Show, Sausalito Arts Festival, and Naples National Arts Festival. She has won several awards, including the Sand Dollar Award at the Virginia Beach Boardwalk Arts Festival, the Tyler School of Art's Faculty Award for Metals, and merit awards at the New Hope Art Festival, the Washington Square Outdoor Art Festival, and the Bethesda Row Art Festival.

MICHAEL AND MAUREEN BANNER
Monterey, Massachusetts
Michael and Maureen Banner run a two-person studio in Monterey, Massachusetts. Michael studied at the Cleveland Institute of Art, Western Michigan University, and Kalamazoo College. Maureen studied at Berkshire Community College, Evanston Art Center, Northern Illinois University, and the Art Institute of Chicago-Junior School. Their work appears in the permanent collections of the Renwick Gallery of the Smithsonian Institution's National Museum of American Art; the Art Institute of Chicago; the Mint Museum of Craft and Design in Charlotte, North Carolina; the Peabody Essex Museum in Salem, Massachusetts; and the Brauer Museum of Art in Valparaiso, Indiana.

MARTHA JO BENSON
Santa Fe, New Mexico
Benson earned a B.A. from Baker University. She studied for five years with silversmith Chuck Evans at Iowa State University and for one year with jeweler Daphne Krinos in London. Her work has appeared in the Lancaster Museum of Art in Lancaster, Pennsylvania; the Schumaker Gallery in Columbus, Ohio, and the Spertus Museum in Chicago where she won the Ceremonial Object award in an international Judaica exhibit. She is represented by the Free Hand Gallery in Los Angeles, California; the Octagon Center for the Arts in Ames, Iowa; and Painter Horse Gallery in Santa Fe, New Mexico. Her work is in the collection of the Northminster Presbyterian Church in Ames, and numerous other private collections.

ALEX BERNARD
Barking, Essex, England
Born in Holland, Bernard studied silversmithing at London Guildhall University, and has worked in New Zealand, Australia, Canada, and the United States. His work has appeared at the Chelsea Crafts Fair, the Royal Cornwall Museum and the Olympia Fine Art and Antiques Fair. The Evening Standard featured him in its Homes and Property section in December 2002. His work is stocked in London by Studio Fusion Gallery, the Gilbert Collection Shop, and Designworks. It is also available on the Web at The Silver Gallery and Objects of Design.

SIGURD BRONGER
Oslo, Norway
www.sigurdbronger.no
Bronger taught at the Royal College of Art in London in 2002, and was trained at the Oslo Goldsmith School. His work appears in the Art Museum of Northern Norway, the Museum of Applied Art in Oslo, the Foundation for Norwegian Arts and Crafts, and several other museums. His work was exhibited in "Nordic Transparency" at the Stedelijk Museum in Amsterdam; "A Matter of Materials" in Canada and the United States; and "Jewelry in the Past/Present/Future" by the Victoria Gallery in Melbourne, Australia. His work can be seen at Gallerie RA in Amsterdam. He is represented in the Museum of Fine Art in Bergen, Trondheim, and Oslo, as well as the Design Museum in Helsinki.

ROBERT COOGAN
Smithville, Tennessee
Coogan studied at Humboldt University and the Cranbrook Academy of Art. He is currently head of the metals department at the Appalachian Center for Crafts, and has taught at Colorado Mountain College, the Center for Creative Studies, and South Devon College of Art and Design. Coogan's work has been exhibited internationally and featured in numerous publications including *American Craft*, *The Anvil's Ring*, *Metalsmith*, and *Korean Design Magazine*.

ANDY COOPERMAN
Seattle, Washington
Cooperman earned a B.A. in studio art from SUNY Oneonta, and has taught at the University of Washington. His work appears in the permanent collection of the Tacoma Art Museum and the collection of Benton Seymour Rabinovitch. He is represented by Patina Gallery in Santa Fe, New Mexico; deNovo Gallery in Palo Alto, California; and the Obsidian Gallery in Tucson, Arizona.

DANIELLE CRISSMAN
Toledo, Ohio
Crissman earned her M.F.A. from Southern Illinois University, Carbondale where she teaches jewelry and metals as a graduate assistant. She is president of the Southern Illinois Metalsmithing Society. Her work has appeared in SIU Carbondale's University Museum and in "Formed to Function?" at the John Michael Kohler Arts Center in Sheboygan, Wisconsin. She has taught workshops and given demonstrations at schools in Kentucky, Maine, North Carolina, and Michigan. Her work has also appeared on the History Channel's "Modern Marvels: Metals."

JACQUELYN A. CRISSMAN
Toledo, Ohio
Crissman is in the graduate program in metalwork at Bowling Green State University in Ohio where she works as a teaching assistant. She won the 2003 Award for Excellence at the Spring Fair in Columbus, Ohio, and first place in applied art at Art on the Mall at the University of Toledo in Ohio. Her work has appeared in the Black Swamp Arts Festival in Bowling Green; the Youngstown State University Summer Festival of the Arts in Ohio; and the Sugarloaf Crafts Festival in Atlanta, Georgia. She is sole proprietor of The Bent Wire in Toledo, Ohio.

JACK P. DA SILVA
Pinole, California
Jack da Silva earned his M.F.A. in metal-smithing and jewelry design from Indiana University in Bloomington, Indiana and his B.A. in jewelry and ceramics from San Jose State University. He teaches at San Francisco City College and the California College of Arts and Crafts in Oakland. He founded MAKER Metal Arts worKshop Retreat in Loma, California, and is owner of Jack da Silva's Metal Design Studio in El Sobrante, California. His work appears in the permanent collections of the Victoria and Albert Museum, the Church of Sao Braz in Portugal, and the Modern Museum of Art in Seoul, South Korea. His work was featured in "Fifty Years in the Making" by the Metal Arts Guild in San Francisco and "Steel City: Contemporary America in Metal" by the Helen T. White Gallery in Pueblo, Colorado.

MARILYN DA SILVA
Pinole, California
Marilyn da Silva earned her M.F.A. in jewelry design and metalsmithing from Indiana University in Bloomington, Indiana and her B.S. in Art Education from Bowling Green State University in Ohio. She is head of the jewelry and metal arts program at the California College of Arts and Crafts in Oakland. Her work appears in the permanent collections of the Decorative Arts Museum of the Arkansas Art Center; the National Ornamental Metal Museum; and the Modern Museum of Art in Seoul, South Korea. Her work was featured in "The Art of Gold" and "Beyond the Mines: the Art of California Gold" at the Crocker Museum in Sacramento, California. Her work has appeared in the publications *Color on Metal* by Tim McCreight and Nicole Bsullack, and *Teapots Transformed: Exploration of an Object* by Leslie Ferrin.

SUSAN R. EWING
Oxford, Ohio
Ewing is head of the metals department at Miami University in Oxford, Ohio. She earned her M.F.A. from Indiana University in Bloomington, Indiana and completed a private study with master silversmith Aldo Vitali of Rome, Italy. She served as a Fulbright Senior Lecturing Scholar at the Academy of Art, Architecture, and Design in Prague from 1997 to 1999. Her work appears in the White House Collection of American Craft at the National Archives in Washington, D.C.; the Alessi Museum in Crusinallo, Italy; and the Indiana University Art Museum. Her work has also appeared in the Los Angeles County Museum of Art, The National Museum of American Art at the Smithsonian Institution, The American Craft Museum, and the Museum für Kunsthandwerks in Frankfurt, Germany.

FRED FENSTER
Sun Prairie, Wisconsin
Fenster teaches at the University of Wisconsin, Madison. He earned his M.F.A. from the Cranbrook Academy of Art in Bloomfield Hills, Michigan. The American Craft Council elected him to the College of Fellows in 1995. His work was featured in "Wisconsin Metalsmiths 1996" by the Villa Terrace Decorative Arts Museum in Milwaukee, Wisconsin. His work appears in the Renwick Gallery of the Smithsonian Institution, the Milwaukee Art Museum, and the National Museum of Contemporary Art in Seoul, South Korea.

YAAKOV GREENVURCEL
Jerusalem, Israel
www.greenvurcel.co.il
Greenvurcel graduated with honors from the Bezalel Academy of Art in Jerusalem, where he won the Shapiro Prize for Judaica for his "Ever Changing Hanukkah Menorah" design. His work has been exhibited by the Bernard Weinger Jewish Community Center in Northbrook, Illinois, and KL Fine Arts in Chicago. His work appears in the permanent collection of museums in Israel, Europe, and the United States, including the Israel Museum in Jerusalem; the Jewish Museum in New York City; the Jewish Museum in Berlin; and the North Carolina Museum of Art in Raleigh.

TIMOTHY LAZURE
Greenville, North Carolina
Lazure teaches metal design at East Carolina University in Greenville, North Carolina. His work has been featured at the Mint Museum of Craft and Design in Charlotte, North Carolina; the 46th Annual National Juried Art Exhibition at the Rock Mount Arts Center in Rocky Mount, North Carolina; the Providence Fine Furnishing Show in Providence, Rhode Island; and at Gallery 224 at the University of Massachusetts in Dartmouth. His work has also appeared in Scotland, London, New Orleans, and San Francisco.

BROOKE MARKS SWANSON
Indianapolis, Indiana
Swanson earned her M.F.A. from the School of Art and Design at the University of Illinois in Urbana-Champaign, where she was a teaching assistant at the University of Illinois. She is currently an Jewelry and Metalsmithing instructor at the Indianapolis Art Center. Her work was featured in "The Bracelet" at Yaw Gallery in New York City; "On the Edge" at the Enamel Exhibition in Olympia, Washington; and the Society of North American Goldsmiths National Juried Student Exhibition in San Francisco. She is a member of the Society of American Silversmiths and the Society of North American Goldsmiths.

RICHARD MAWDSLEY
Carbondale, Illinois
Mawdsley is a professor at Southern Illinois University, Carbondale. His work appears in the Museum of Fine Arts in Boston, Yale University Art Gallery, the American Crafts Museum in New York City, and the Renwick Gallery of the Smithsonian Institution. He is a fellow of the American Craft Council, and his work was featured in "Generating Connections: Emerging Jewelry Artists and Mentors" at the Society of Arts and Crafts in Boston; "Attitude and Action! North American Figurative Jewelry" at the University of Central England, Birmingham Institute of Art and Design; and DESIGNyard in Dublin, Ireland.

PEGEEN MILLER-KERN
Fort Wayne, Indiana

Miller-Kern earned her M.F.A. in metals from Bowling Green State University in Ohio and her B.F.A. in crafts and graphic design from Indiana University. She currently teaches at Indiana University at Fort Wayne. Her work has appeared in the Steinbaum-Krauss Gallery in New York City, the Fort Wayne Museum of Art, the Toledo Museum of Art, the Mansfield Art Center in Mansfield, Ohio, and the Ohio Craft Museum in Columbus.

THOMAS P. MUIR
Perrysburg, Ohio

Muir currently teaches at Bowling Green State University in Ohio, and taught at the Center for Creative Design in Detroit, Michigan. He earned his M.F.A. in jewelry and metalsmithing from Indiana University. He is a past president of the Michigan Silversmiths Guild, and a member of the Society of North American Goldsmiths. His work is in the permanent collection of the Art Institute of Chicago and the National Air and Space Museum of the Smithsonian Institution.

KEVIN O'DWYER
County Offaly, Ireland
www.millennium2000silver.com

O'Dwyer studied at the Art Institute of Chicago. He completed apprenticeships with Harriet Dreissigger in jewelry and enamel, and with William Frederick in silversmithing. He is an artist initiator for the Lough Boora Sculpture Symposium in Ireland. His work has appeared in the Slidell Cultural Center in Slidell, Louisiana; Hibernia in Neptune Beach, Florida; and the J. Cotter Gallery in Vail, Colorado. His work is in the permanent collection of the High Museum in Atlanta, the Ulster Museum in Belfast, and the collection of United States President Bill Clinton. He is represented by the Ferrin Gallery in Lenox, Massachusetts; Hibernia in Neptune Beach, Florida; J. Cotter Gallery in Vail, Colorado; and Nauda in Chicago, Illinois.

CAROLANNE PATTERSON
New York, New York

Patterson earned her M.F.A. and B.F.A. from SUNY, New Paltz, and she earned a B.A. in art history from the University of Pittsburgh. She teaches in the metals department at New York University. Her work was featured in "Behind the Glass Door" at New York University; "Dog Show" at the John Michael Kohler Arts Center in Sheboygan, Wisconsin; and in solo exhibitions in New York City and San Diego. She won the New York Foundation for the Arts Fellowship in 2001. Her work has also appeared in *Mountain Bike Magazine* and *Primordial Undermine*.

SARAH PERKINS
Springfield, Missouri

Perkins earned her M.F.A. from Southern Illinois University, Carbondale, and she teaches metals at Southwest Missouri State University in Springfield. Her work appears in Mobilia Gallery in Cambridge, Massachusetts, and Studio Fusion Gallery in London. Her work was part of the "Color and Light International Enamel Exhibition" in New Delhi and Bombay, India; and "Steel City: Contemporary America in Metal" in Pueblo, Colorado. Her work is in the permanent collections of the Decorative Arts College in the Brooklyn Museum of Art; the National Ornamental Metal Museum; and the Evansville Museum of Arts and Sciences.

G. PHIL POIRIER
San Cristobal, New Mexico

Poirier teaches courses in advanced metalsmithing techniques each summer at the Taos Institute of Arts in Taos, New Mexico. He has also taught jewelry classes for the Taos Pueblo, the Santa Fe School of Metalsmithing, and for the Society of North American Goldsmiths conference workshop series. Poirier was one of five artists invited to The University of New Mexico Harwood Museum exhibit, "Objects, Five Master Craftsmen." His work appears in the Emily Benoist Ruffin Goldsmiths Gallery in Taos, New Mexico; Tops in Malibu, California; Mesa's Edge in Taos Ski Valley, New Mexico; and the N.W. Barrett Gallery in Portsmouth, New Hampshire.

RUTH RHOTEN
Oakland, California

Rhoten studied silversmithing in Ireland and metal sculpture at the Soborg School in Copenhagen. She worked as a sheet metal apprentice at the Todds Shipyard in Seattle. She taught in San Francisco at the California Institute of Integral Studies and the San Francisco Art Institute. Her work appears in the collections of Bianca Jaggar; Larry Ellison, CEO of Oracle; the Jungian Institute in San Francisco; and Jay Kensner, medicineman of the Wintu Tribe in Mount Shasta, California. Her work has been exhibited by the Craftsmans' Guild and Shreves and Company in San Francisco, and the Sculpture Exhibition of the Soborg School.

REBECCA SCHEER
Portland, Oregon

Scheer teaches at the Oregon College of Art and Craft in Portland, and earned her M.F.A. from the University of Oregon in Eugene. Her work was featured in "Formed to Function?" at the John Michael Kohler Gallery in Sheboygan, Wisconsin; "big LITTLE" in Oakland, California; "Display Use Only" in Kirkland, Washington; the "2003 Craft Biennial" at the Oregon College of Art and Craft; and the Portland Institute for Contemporary Art, as well as in several private collections.

LISA SLOVIS
San Diego, California
www.lisaslovis.com

Slovis earned her M.F.A. from San Diego University and her B.F.A. from the University of Wisconsin, Madison. She teaches design dynamics at the Coronado School of the Arts in Coronado, California, and also teaches at Southwestern Community College in Chula Vista, California. Her work has been published in *The New York Times*, *Giftware News*, and the *Oakland Press*. Her exhibits include the Beverly Hills Affair in the Gardens; the American Craft Council Show in Baltimore; and the Scottsdale Arts Festival in Scottsdale, Arizona.

BARRY THOMAS
Bradley Ashbourne, England
Thomas won first prize in silversmithing from the British Jewelers' Association in 1999 and 2000. His work is included in the collections of St. Catherine's College in Cambridge, the Duchess of Devonshire, and Benton Seymour Rabinovitch. His work has been exhibited in the goldsmith's fair at the Goldsmith's Hall in London; "Art in Action" at Waterperry, Oxfordshire; and "Common Ground" at the Chatsworth House.

PAMELA MORRIS THOMFORD
Perrysburg, Ohio
Thomford studied ceramics at the University of Toledo in Ohio, and metalsmithing at Bowling Green University in Ohio. She appears in the book *Art Jewelry Today* by Dona Meilach, and is represented by Nancy Yaw Gallery in Birmingham, Michigan. Her work was featured in "Refined III: Small Forms in Precious Metal" at the Griffith Gallery in Nacogdoches, Texas and "Contemporary Works of Faith '03" at the Schumacher Gallery in Columbus, Ohio. Her work has also appeared in "Consuming Passion: Edible by Design" at the Arts Castle in Delaware, Ohio and the "Liturgical Art Show" at the Ann Arbor Art Center.

SADIE SHU PING WANG
Silver Point, Tennessee
Wang earned her M.F.A. from the Cranbrook Academy of Art in Bloomfield Hills, Michigan. She was an artist-in-residence at the Appalachian Center for Craft at the Tennessee Technological University in 1999. Her work appears in the permanent collection "Birmingham Memories" at the National Taiwan Craft Research Institute. Her work was featured at the Appalachian Center for Craft; in "Craft Forms 2001" at the Wayne Art Center in Wayne, Pennsylvania; and in the "37th Mid-States Craft Exhibition" at the Evansville Museum of Art and Science in Evansville Indiana.

PAUL WELLER
Benalla, Australia
Weller earned his B.F.A. in goldsmithing and silversmithing from the Royal Melbourne Institute of Technology. He works as a silversmith for Mewo Metal Products in the fabrication of architectural metal fittings. His work has appeared at the Walker St. Gallery of the Dandenong Community Arts Center in Dandenong, Victoria, Australia; "Class of '95" at the Goldsmith Hall in London; and "Fluid Mechanics" at the Customs House in Melbourne, Australia. He won the Klepner Award in Limited Series Production and the Tanzer Award in Silversmithing Design, both from the Royal Melbourne Institute of Technology.

JULIA WOODMAN
Atlanta, Georgia
Woodman was a Fulbright Scholar in Lahti, Finland, where she became the first American certified as a master silversmith in that country. She earned her M.F.A. from Georgia State University in Atlanta. She teaches at the Penland School of Crafts in Penland, North Carolina; and at the Spruill Center for Arts and the Chastain Arts Center, both in Atlanta, Georgia. Her work has been featured at the Penland School Gallery and the Signature Gallery in Atlanta. She is represented by the Bascom Louise Gallery in Highlands, North Carolina.

YOSHIKO YAMAMOTO
Boston, Massachusetts
Yamamoto's work is included in the permanent collection of the Museum of Fine Arts in Boston. Her work as has been featured by the Canadian Clay and Glass Gallery in Waterloo, Canada; the Nancy Yaw Gallery in Birmingham, Michigan; Galleria Mesa in Mesa City, Arizona; and Mobilia Gallery in Cambridge, Massachusetts. She teaches enameling, metalforming, and jewelry at the School of the Museum of Fine Arts in Boston.

VALENTIN YOTKOV
Morganville, New Jersey
Yotkov graduated from the Specialized Art School in Sofia, Bulgaria, and apprenticed under Bulgarian silversmith Alexander Raiev. He has taught workshops at the Syracuse University School of Art and Design in Syracuse, New York; the Denver Jewelry Academy in Denver, Colorado; and the Revere Academy of Jewelry Arts in San Francisco, California. His work has been featured at the SFA Gallery in Nacogdoches, Texas; SOFA New York; and the Lauren Stanley Gallery in New York. He won first prize in the National Art Show in Sofia, Bulgaria. He is a member of the Society of American Silversmiths and the National Silversmiths Guild of Bulgaria.

Templates

Business Card Holder, page 59

Baby Spoon, page 66

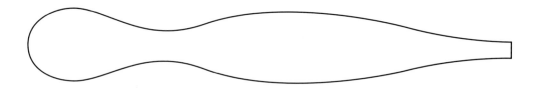

Condiment Dish, page 76

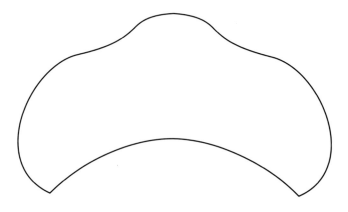

Pie Server

Spatula

TEMPLATES

Acknowledgments

Many people made this book possible.

Thanks to Steve Mann, my photographer, Kristi Pfeffer, my art director, and Chris Bryant—a fantastic visual team that can make even scrap metal look good.

Thanks to Marthe Le Van, my editor.

Thanks to Nathalie Mornu, my assistant editor.

Thanks to Carol Taylor, Deborah Morgenthal, and Terry Taylor for finding me and sponsoring this project.

Thanks to the people and friends who put up with me during the creation of this book.

Lastly, and with great sentiment (and if I ever hear the end of this it will be a miracle), thanks to my mother for her support over the years. Your love is like a hammer—not always pretty, surely not always gentle, but without it the metal wouldn't move.

For all of those listed above, the silver would not shine as bright without your help. Thank you all.

Index

INDEX, SUPPLIERS, ARTIST INDEX

Notes on Suppliers
Usually, the supplies you need for making the projects in Lark books can be found at your local craft supply store, discount mart, home improvement center, or retail shop relevant to the topic of the book. Occasionally, however, you may need to buy materials or tools from specialty suppliers. In order to provide you with the most up-to-date information, we have created a listing of suppliers on our website, which we update on a regular basis. Visit us at www.larkbooks.com; click on "Craft Supply Sources"; and then click on the relevant topic. You will find numerous companies listed with their website address and/or mailing address and phone number.

GALLERY ARTIST INDEX